IOOF *to* Insignia Financial

IOOF *to* Insignia Financial

The story of a friendly society that grew into a financial powerhouse

Engel Schmidl

ALLEN&UNWIN
SYDNEY•MELBOURNE•AUCKLAND•LONDON

Allen & Unwin
Cammeraygal Country
83 Alexander Street
Crows Nest NSW 2065
Australia
Phone: (61 2) 8425 0100
Email: info@allenandunwin.com
Web: www.allenandunwin.com

*Allen & Unwin acknowledges the Traditional Owners of the Country on which we
live and work. We pay our respects to all Aboriginal and Torres Strait Islander
Elders, past and present.*

A catalogue record for this
book is available from the
National Library of Australia

ISBN 978 1 76147 051 6

Index by Puddingburn
Set in 11.5/13.5 pt Janson by Midland Typesetters, Australia
Printed and bound in China by 1010 Printing Ltd

10 9 8 7 6 5 4 3 2 1

The paper in this book is FSC® certified.
FSC® promotes environmentally responsible,
socially beneficial and economically viable
management of the world's forests.

CONTENTS

FOREWORD

Whilst Insignia Financial is a relatively new brand in the Australian landscape, it is a company with decades of proud and, at times, tumultuous history. Founded in 1846 as the Independent Order of Odd Fellows to protect working families, the company has continued to focus on putting clients first, by understanding their needs and helping them to secure their financial future. As the company's current Chairman, I can attest to this purpose and ambition remaining a constant, despite the company growing and evolving.

The last time the company's history was thoroughly documented was some 30 years ago. Geoffrey Blainey, highly respected Australian historian and academic, wrote a book—*Odd Fellows: A history of IOOF Australia*—which covered the rich history until the end of the 1980s, with a strong focus on the first century of the organisation's evolution. Given the company's growth and changes in the new millennium, it was time to revisit and update the story. We invited Engel Schmidl—an experienced journalist who has written for publications such as *SmartCompany, INTHEBLACK, The Saturday Paper* and others—to tell our story anew.

Over the past few years Engel has spent hours interviewing former and current employees and leaders, and spoken to more than 20 people, including former CEOs and chairs. He also scoured annual reports, archive material and thousands of newspaper articles to source insights into what has made this ASX 200 company perform and why it has survived significant disruptions and changes, especially over the past 40 years. The breadth and depth of this research have resulted in an informative, engaging and inspirational read on one of Australia's oldest financial institutions.

From inception as the Independent Order of Odd Fellows in Melbourne, to membership numbers significantly increasing during the 1870s and 1880s, to the introduction of pharmacy dispensaries to service members in 1946, to being close to insolvency in 1978, to the first non-odd fellow CEO appointment in 1982, to becoming Australia's biggest friendly society in the late 1990s, to listing on the ASX in 2003 and to more recent events such as the acquisitions of the MLC and ANZ pensions and investments businesses, the book covers many significant events in the company's history.

What is apparent as one reads the book is that culture has always played an important part in shaping the organisation. External factors such as the political and competitive environment, the regulatory requirements, and technological changes have all contributed to forming our culture—as have internal factors, such as the composition and quality of our employees, company structure, and the strength of leadership. Culture and a strong sense of purpose are what have helped the company rebound and advance.

Insignia Financial is at another juncture at present, as current CEO Renato Mota transitions out of the business. A new chapter will start with the new CEO, and that story is yet to be told—but as a custodian of a business with a 175 year plus heritage, the new leader will be well aware of the legacy created by those that came before.

Allan Griffiths
Chairman
Insignia Financial Ltd

December 2023

PREFACE

This book came about after extensive discussions with former Insignia Financial CEO Renato Mota and former Insignia Financial executive and director Tony Hodges. Without them, this project would not have happened.

Renato and Tony wanted me to go beyond dates and events to capture the spirit of Insignia Financial, an organisation they both care about deeply. They also wanted the organisation's history updated to include the momentous events of the past 30 years or so since the publication of the original Insignia Financial history book, *Odd Fellows: A History of IOOF Australia*.

The first book was written by the highly esteemed Professor Geoffrey Blainey, an Australian historian with few peers. His work provides the bedrock for this one. This book builds upon his work by re-examining the past through a new lens and recontextualising some of it for an audience that may not be familiar with terms and concepts such as fraternal order, friendly society and mutual benefits.

This book also brings the story up to date, encompassing the many momentous events that have shaped the organisation and led to it becoming Insignia Financial in 2021. I hope I've done some justice to the first book's legacy and Renato and Tony's wishes to document the organisation's proud and rich story.

I'd like to thank Renato and Tony for their help, guidance and encouragement throughout the writing of the book. Tony's place in the Insignia Financial story is unique, and his stories and insights provided me with so much more than just the bare bones of a chronology of events.

I'd like to thank all those I interviewed for their time, patience and goodwill. Their stories enliven this book and bring a human dimension to what otherwise could have been a dry recounting of a corporate history. I would also like to mention the support provided by employees at Insignia Financial, especially Alina Burdajewicz, who kept me on track during this project.

Lastly, a big thank you to my wife Jess and children Alby and Ruby. Their love and support mean the world to me.

Engel Schmidl

The Melbourne-based Independent Order of Odd Fellows was founded in 1846. Over the next century, lodges would be established around Australia, including this group in Albury, NSW. Mitchell Library, State Library of New South Wales

CHAPTER 1

A NEW NAME WITH A RICH HISTORY

❋

On 25 November 2021, a new name was introduced to the Australian business landscape. That day, Insignia Financial Ltd (Insignia Financial) assumed its place in the top 200 companies listed on the Australian Securities Exchange (ASX), with nearly $300 billion in funds under management and administration. An ambitious, growing business, Insignia Financial's mission is to help Australians secure their financial future. Its purpose: 'Understand me, look after me, secure my future.'[1]

However, Insignia Financial was not an entirely new organisation. Its history dates back to 1846, with the founding of the Duke of York Lodge, affiliated with the Independent Order of Odd Fellows (IOOF) friendly society. That makes Insignia Financial one of the oldest financial institutions in Australia. Its founding was not a grand affair: friends meeting in a Melbourne pub. Victoria was not yet a state. Australia was still 55 years away from becoming a nation.

For the next 150 years or so, friendly societies like IOOF provided Australians with many of the social and financial services governments did not offer. Funeral funds, medical insurance, and sickness and injury allowances were among the basic financial needs covered by the friendly societies, which were also known as mutual aid societies.

Times changed and the financial services industry evolved, but IOOF always maintained its purpose to look after the financial wellbeing of its members. That mission lives on with Insignia Financial and remains at the core of its business.

Insignia Financial was created by merging IOOF with the MLC and ANZ wealth-management businesses. IOOF acquired substantial parts of ANZ's OnePath Pensions and Investments (ANZ P&I) business and the ANZ-aligned dealer groups in January 2020. Midway through 2020, IOOF announced its acquisition of the MLC business from NAB. Through these acquisitions, IOOF became the country's largest retail wealth-management firm and among the most significant organisations in the financial services industry.[2]

Each of the three businesses that merged to create Insignia Financial has a unique and proud history. MLC started life in 1886 as the Citizens' Assurance Company Limited headquartered in Melbourne. That company amalgamated with the Mutual Life Association of Australasia in 1908, becoming known as the Mutual

Life and Citizens' Assurance Company Limited.[3] The ANZ wealth-management businesses can trace their lineage to Mercantile Mutual, which was established in 1878 and acquired by the Dutch banking group ING in 2001. All three groups—IOOF, MLC and Mercantile Mutual—contributed substantially to business life in Australia and the broader community.

Over the years, Insignia Financial acquired a number of organisations, including Australian Wealth Management, Skandia, the Order of the Sons of Temperance (OST) and the Hibernian Australasian Catholic Benefit Society, all of which have contributed to the company's rich tapestry.

Former Insignia Financial CEO Renato Mota joined IOOF in 2003. He was immediately struck by the organisation's significant legacy and the stories from its past he heard from colleagues like Tony Hodges, an iconic figure within IOOF and someone held in high regard in the financial services industry.

'There's certainly a strong sense of history in the organisation,' Mota said when interviewed for this book, which updates and extends the history of IOOF previously written by the esteemed Australian historian Geoffrey Blainey.[4] Professor Blainey's book concludes in 1990, and much has happened since then.

A group of Masters and Officers of the Independent Order of Odd Fellows (IOOF) in Sydney. Mitchell Library, State Library of New South Wales

Mota said knowing the organisation's history gave him a keener insight into its mission:

~

I think the history of the organisation gives us confidence and courage. That's probably where the source of courage comes from: we will keep doing what we've always done: listening to our clients, making brave but sensible calls and living to fight another day.

It's something we talk a lot about, and the fact that we're custodians of this. It was here well before we were here, it'll be here after us, and we owe it to all the stakeholders, past and present and future, to leave it in better shape than when we found it.

~

A recurring theme of the organisation's history, noted by many of those interviewed for this book, is its capacity for change. Said Mota:

~

IOOF always had this amazing willingness to face into change, whether it was acquiring OST in 1990 or, more recently, with the acquisition of MLC. Its history gives you the sense of an organisation that listened to its members and was never so set in its ways that it couldn't find a way to respond to its members' demands and the world around it.

~

According to Mota, the spirit of change and the resilience to move with the times live on with Insignia Financial:

~

It's not a self-fulfilling prophecy. Sitting here and talking about it isn't going to make it happen. We can't just think that IOOF managed to survive the last 175 years, therefore, we will survive, too. We bear witness to that history, but we must always keep an eye on the future.

~

He said that a profound sense of purpose is abundantly visible within Insignia Financial and its work to help Australians secure their financial wellbeing:

~

That gives us confidence that we have a legitimate claim on this territory of financial wellbeing because it's what this organisation has always done. We think the opportunity is there, and we think our heritage gives us the right to play in this space and that all manifests in the culture and the actions of our people.

~

As of December 2023, Insignia Financial counts around 2 million Australians as clients of its products and services. Headquartered in Melbourne, it has offices in Sydney, Wollongong, Adelaide, Brisbane, Perth and Hobart, and around 4700 employees.

The Insignia Financial business comprises three primary service areas: platforms, advice and asset management.

The platforms business enables Insignia Financial to be one of Australia's largest super fund and pension providers, offering a wide range of award-winning solutions. A robust and contemporary technology platform demonstrates Insignia Financial's ongoing commitment to investing in technology and services to support clients' changing needs. Total funds under administration across Insignia Financial's platforms total $205.5 billion.[5]

Insignia Financial is passionate about the role financial advice can play in the lives of all Australians. Its extensive network of advisers provides financial advice options—from guidance and coaching to episodic and holistic advice based on client needs. The network includes two employed groups, Bridges and Shadforth, alongside a number of self-employed advice businesses under licence—RI Advice, Millennium3, Lonsdale, Godfrey Pembroke and Consultum—and self-licensed services such as IOOF Alliances. Insignia Financial's advice offering continues to transform under a new sustainable advice model to improve client engagement and the efficiency of advice practices. There are around 1385 advisers in the Insignia Financial network.[6]

As a wealth manager, Insignia Financial has built on the success of IOOF, MLC and the ANZ asset management businesses. It applies

Dispensation certificates were issued by the head office of a friendly society to record and commemorate the lodge's membership of an order. National Gallery of Australia

its knowledge and experience to deliver the best possible investment results for institutional and retail clients in Australia and globally. It offers access to a broad suite of investment capabilities across various multi-asset and single-asset classes. Its investment management is driven by over 100 investment professionals in Australia, the United States and the United Kingdom. It has $87.6 billion in funds under management.[7]

Mota said the past few years have been turbulent at times. In 2018, IOOF faced critical questioning at the Royal Commission into Misconduct in the Banking, Superannuation and Financial Services Industry. Following that, the COVID-19 pandemic played out as IOOF was bedding down the acquisition of the ANZ P&I businesses while acquiring MLC. These challenges tested the resources and resolve of the organisation and its employees.

For Mota and Insignia Financial chair Allan Griffiths, reconnecting the organisation to its spirit and purpose was vital during this time. Importantly, it was not a matter of finding the organisation's purpose; that was already there. Said Mota:

~

We didn't define that purpose; I didn't define it; it was defined by the founders and those who have created a path and a tapestry. My view is that we need to stitch into that tapestry, and it goes to that concept of being custodians of the business. We very deliberately describe ourselves as an every-person organisation. We're not an elitist organisation; we're not for the rich and famous; we are an every-person organisation, just as it was in 1846. We will continue to grow by delivering financial wellbeing for all Australians.

~

Insignia Financial's history is a remarkable tale of adaptability, resilience and success.

The IOOF were not the only Odd Fellows. Other Odd Fellows organisations included the Manchester Unity Independent Order of Odd Fellows and the Grand United Order of Odd Fellows. City of Coffs Harbour

CHAPTER 2

THE ORIGIN OF
FRIENDLY SOCIETIES

❋

Insignia Financial has an unusual history. Its origins run deeper than many realise, with plenty of twists and turns. The company now known as Insignia Financial started in 1846 at a pub called the Waterman's Arms, on Little Collins Street near the corner of Elizabeth Street in Melbourne. Here, a lodge of the friendly society named the Independent Order of Odd Fellows established itself in a frontier town, a colonial outpost of the British Empire, to provide fellowship and financial security.

Those who met at the Waterman's Arms on 13 October 1846 established the Duke of York Lodge, which followed the Oddfellowship traditions of the Independent Order of Odd Fellows. Why were these fellows odd? They were odd because they didn't belong to professional associations or trade and crafts guilds. They were often self-employed, sole traders, merchants or small-business people: butchers, bakers and candlestick makers. They were not the landed gentry, but nor were they destitute. They were fellows because they shared a camaraderie: they stood shoulder to shoulder, individuals who together formed a community. Before social welfare, this fellowship provided economic support and an extended network of social care.

An example of the Odd Fellows insignia that was once a common sight on buildings in towns around Australia, as seen on Lithgow Union Theatre (formerly the Odd Fellows Hall). Photo by Samantha Kent

Terms like *fraternal order, friendly society* and *mutual aid organisation* are not commonplace today. Context is required to understand who those intrepid odd fellows were, what they set out to do and the world in which they lived.

The Collins dictionary definition of 'fraternal order' is 'a society, often secret, of members banded together for mutual benefit or for work toward a common goal'. In this context, the Freemasons immediately come to mind. Their sense of structure and hierarchy, and even their penchant for things like secret passwords, were common to fraternal orders. Indeed, friendly societies like IOOF often modelled themselves on the Freemasons.

Friendly societies are a subset of fraternal orders. They are mutual benefit organisations in which members pay into funds covering specific needs, most commonly sickness funds, death benefits and funeral funds. Such societies enabled working people to pool their resources and provide for themselves at a time when government welfare barely existed. They catered to the emerging working and middle classes created by industrialisation, and were both social and financial clubs.

According to the *Dr Bob James Fraternal Societies Collection*, 'The ultimate aim and function of these networks were preserving a working-class person's respectability through keeping out of poverty.'[1]

A ceremonial collar traditionally worn by IOOF Grand Nobles and Grand Masters. Courtesy of Chris Meneilly, photo by Joanne Ho and George Stajsic

Medals bestowed on IOOF members for loyalty and service created a sense of identity, belonging and community. Courtesy of Chris Meneilly, photo by Joanne Ho and George Stajsic

The secret passwords, elaborate initiation rituals and ceremonies, aprons and silk gowns of fraternal orders dressed up their primary function, which was to provide working people with financial security.

'Oddfellowship' is an umbrella term that embraces several fraternal orders, the largest of which, in the early to mid-1800s, were the Manchester Unity Independent Order of Odd Fellows (MUIOOF) and the Grand United Order of Odd Fellows (GUOOF). The Independent Order of Odd Fellows (sometimes known as the Ancient Independent Order of Odd Fellows) was part of this broader group. The Oddfellowship societies developed in the United Kingdom in the mid-1700s, eventually spreading in popularity globally, especially in the British colonies.

Whilst some historians claim that friendly societies dated to Roman times, the consensus is that the concept of mutual aid dates to the mid-1500s in the form of 'box clubs', informal associations for agricultural and seasonal workers. David Green and Lawrence Cromwell write:

~

As we know them today, friendly societies originated in Britain during the eighteenth century, although some were founded earlier. The oldest, the Incorporation of Carters, was founded in 1555 at Leith in Scotland. The second oldest, the United General Sea Box of Borrowstounness, was founded in 1634.[2]

~

Robinson Crusoe author Daniel Defoe was an early advocate. In *An Essay upon Projects*, published in 1697 and focusing on societies for sailors and widows, he defines friendly societies as 'a number of people entering into a mutual compact to help one another in case any disaster or distress fall upon them'. He viewed the friendly society's motivating concerns as financial security, friendship and good health. His premise for friendly societies reveals the harsh conditions of life at the time:

~

Man is the worst of all God's creatures to shift for himself; no other animal is ever starved to death; nature without has provided them both food and clothes, and nature within has placed an instinct that never fails to direct them to proper means for a supply; but man must either work or starve, slave or die. He has indeed reason given him to direct him, and few who follow the dictates of that reason come to such unhappy exigencies; but when by the errors of a man's youth he has reduced himself to such a degree of distress as to be absolutely without three things—money, friends, and health—he dies in a ditch, or in some worse place, a hospital.[3]

~

The spectre of death in that age was never far away. Historian Geoffrey Blainey writes in his definitive *Odd Fellows: A History of IOOF Australia*: 'Death ranked high in the thoughts and ceremonies of the Odd Fellows. The unexpectedness of death and the hardship it caused in a more austere era was perhaps the main reason for the existence and popularity of these lodges.'[4]

Early friendly societies attempted to create identity, community and stability amid precarious times. Pre-modern, medieval communities gave way to a new set of dynamics: the mobility of men, money and markets. Capitalism was emerging. Friendly societies were one response to this new world.

In *Trust among Strangers: Friendly Societies in Modern Britain*, Penelope Ismay has written that friendly societies mediated their members' social and economic concerns:

~

The concept and practice of [the] friendly society was, in fact, a robust and nimble cultural resource for thinking about and working through some of the most pressing questions facing British society in a period marked by rapid social and economic change. Questions about what people in a society owe to each other are foundational—the answers structure and legitimate social order. The reciprocity that one comes to expect from others, and the conditions under which those expectations are met, produce the diffuse bonds of social trust that hold societies together.[5]

~

Friendly societies intertwined their members' social and economic interests. The theatricality with which they did this might appear quaint to sophisticated citizens of globalised, postmodern societies. Still, symbols, costumes, passwords, ceremonies and even secret handshakes helped create a space for building trust between people. The diligent stewardship of members' funds consolidated that trust. The social and the financial went hand in hand, in circles of friendship linked much like IOOF's logo.

Fraternal orders, friendly societies and mutual aid still exist. Insignia Financial can trace its origins to them, even if it's not any of those things today. The genetic markers remain. However, the crucial role friendly societies once played has receded. The rise of state welfare and the proliferation of different kinds of non-bank financial institutions diminished their place and standing throughout the 20th century.

These days, friendly societies live in the popular consciousness mainly through the landmark architecture associated with many orders. We occasionally look up and see a symbol or inscription—like the Odd Fellows' all-seeing eye, or the motto 'Love, Friendship and Truth'—on a stately building, and faintly recognise its provenance. Likewise, the more mysterious 'secret' elements of the old orders persist, although they are nowhere near as prevalent as even a

Friendly societies assertively advertised their benefits to prospective members. University of Newcastle, Australia

century ago. These relics tell us little about what friendly societies did or how they helped people of limited financial means secure a better life. The friendly society legacy lives through those they supported through good times, but especially the bad.

Friendly societies like the Independent Order of Odd Fellows helped members navigate an often unfriendly world, socially and financially. They provided sanctuary and assurance. For most of us, history now cloaks the purpose and existence of the friendly society and its vital importance. Societal transformations meant the economy became more complex, technological and globalised. Institutions adapted and transformed to meet new demands. Those friendly societies that could not respond faded, while others evolved.

In 1846, then, when William Clarke, a well-respected member of the community an a compositor on the *Port Phillip Herald*, met with friends at a pub in Melbourne, the organisation they were establishing would aim to ensure its members could look after themselves and their families. The business known as Insignia Financial today is significantly different to the organisation Clarke and his odd fellows founded. Yet its spirit aligns with those of the men who met at the Waterman's Arms all those years ago. The goalposts for financial wellbeing have shifted over time, but the desire of everyday men and women to provide for their loved ones and themselves endures.

The economic downturn of the 1890s led to widespread poverty in cities like Melbourne. Friendly society membership helped keep many afloat. M&N/Alamy

CHAPTER 3

FRIENDSHIP,
LOVE AND TRUTH

※

The first public sign of the Independent Order of Odd Fellows group that would eventually become Insignia Financial was an advertisement in several Melbourne newspapers in late September and early October 1846. The ad suggests that the members of the fledgling society had already met, most likely as part of another Odd Fellows group started in Melbourne in 1840.

The first group's founders in 1840 were D.A. Strode and George Arden. Known as the Australia Felix Lodge of the Independent Order of Odd Fellows, this lodge later joined the Manchester Unity Independent Order of Odd Fellows. Strode and Arden's group had links to an Odd Fellows lodge established in Sydney in 1836. The story goes that Strode and Arden thought they were establishing a Melbourne branch of the Manchester Unity lodge, but learned later that the Sydney lodge had no chartered link to the UK-based Manchester Unity. A few years later, another group, the Grand United Order of Odd Fellows, would spring up in Melbourne.

There is little evidence to indicate why William Clarke and his odd fellows left the Strode and Arden group, but it was not unusual for societies to split or for rebel lodges to be established. That meeting at the Waterman's Arms Hotel set in train the remarkable story that would one day culminate in the creation of Insignia Financial.

The ad read:

~

Ancient and Independent Order of Odd Fellows

The Brethren of the above Order are respectfully requested to meet at the Melbourne Duke of York Lodge Rooms, held at the Waterman's Arms, Little Collins Street, on Tuesday evening next, October 13th, on business of importance, at seven o'clock. By order of the n.g. [Noble Grand].[1]

~

Two months later, the *Port Phillip Herald* (the progenitor of Melbourne's long-running *Herald* newspaper, and the present-day *Herald Sun*) reported on 23 December 1846 what seemed to be the order's first annual dinner:

Oddfellowship

The Duke of York Lodge of the Independent Order of Odd Fellows met together on Saturday evening at Host Dunbell's, Waterman's Arms, Little Collins Street, and spent what might be termed a happy evening. Invitations had been previously transmitted to his Worship the Mayor and the editors of the local journals. At seven o'clock about thirty-six of the brethren assembled, when a sumptuous supper was served up, after which a dessert, all the fruits being the products of Australia Felix. Letters of apology for non-attendance were read from His Worship the Mayor, and Mr Cavenagh, of the Port Phillip Herald, the latter of whom requested to have himself enrolled as a member on the next night of meeting.[2]

~

William Clarke, the first Noble Grand of IOOF, was a compositor on the *Port Phillip Herald*, which might explain why Mayor Cavenagh joined. An influential Melbourne identity, Cavenagh was also the founder and publisher of the *Herald*. A report in the *Port Phillip Gazette and Settler's Journal* mentions that 'the company did ample justice to the cheer'. It continues:

~

. . . in giving some of the toasts, they said that the founders of the lodge were only five in number, and now it numbered about fifty members within the short space of ten weeks. That it was still increasing and likely to equal any Lodge, both for numbers and respectability in the Town . . . The company did not separate until within a short time of midnight when they quietly departed to their homes much gratified with the proceedings.[3]

~

Yet those early years were not without controversy. The rival local Manchester Unity Independent Order of Odd Fellows often castigated the upstart Duke of York Lodge in the local press for not being authentic Odd Fellows:

Loyal Independent Order of Odd Fellows Belonging to Manchester Unity

The members of the Order of Odd Fellows of the Port Phillip District, acting under and in compliance with the MANCHESTER UNITY, find it necessary to point out in this public manner, that the very numerous body to which they belong, is in NO WAY connected with a Society which has recently been announced in the Melbourne journals, under a somewhat similar designation . . . the Lodges of the Unity acting under dispensations from the Parent Lodge at Manchester, DO NOT IN THE MOST REMOTE MANNER ACKNOWLEDGE OR RECOGNISE ANY OTHER SOCIETY using the name of Odd Fellows, NOR ALLOW SUCH PARTIES TO PARTICIPATE IN ANY OF THE BENEFITS OR ADVANTAGES OF LODGES BELONGING TO THE MANCHESTER UNITY . . .[4]

~

The building of the IOOF Hall in Russell Street, Melbourne, aided the exposure of the organisation as its popularity grew in the late 1800s. State Library of Victoria

Blainey surmised that the Duke of York Lodge was started by 'disgruntled people who had preferred to resign from the Australia Felix Lodge rather than live under the umbrella of Manchester Unity.'[5] Those who started up lodges tended to be strong-willed people with their own vision on how things should be run. It's quite possible that was the case in this scenario.[6]

Mergers, splits and takeovers were common among friendly societies. They were organisations made up of people who invested time, money and effort into running them, almost always voluntarily. Egos clashed, principles conflicted and a touch of skulduggery occasionally crept in. Scandals had emerged around that time in England regarding fraudulent behaviour by a senior Manchester Unity official who had embezzled a large sum from the order. The idealistic talk of brotherhood went hand in hand with pragmatic wariness to ensure members' funds were handled properly. Trust was paramount, and improprieties often led to members exiting one society for another.

According to friendly society historian Dr Bob James, this rivalry usually revolved around claims to legitimacy: 'Winning the competitive situation meant achieving legitimacy as the "real" odd fellows.'[7] The rivalries often attracted press commentary. In *The Chronicles of Early Melbourne 1835–1852*, first published in 1888, author 'Garryowen' elaborates:

~

In 1846, there was started in Melbourne a branch of the Duke of York Ancient and Independent Order of Oddfellows, and their motto was 'Friendship, Love, and Truth', a triad which, certainly, so far as the first two elements were concerned, was occasionally transgressed as regarded the Manchester Unity, with which a spirited, and sometimes rather over-brisk rivalry was prosecuted.[8]

~

In 1846, Melbourne was a southern outpost of the Colony of Port Phillip. Established only eleven years earlier, it was a rough-and-tumble place with more huts than houses. IOOF grew slowly in its first few years. The competition was fierce for members among societies, such as the United Ancient Order of Druids (formed in 1851, also at the Waterman's Arms) and the Ancient Order of Foresters (established in Victoria in 1849).

The discovery of gold in 1850 permanently changed the sleepy township. Melbourne became the capital of the newly proclaimed Colony of Victoria, which gained independence from New South Wales on 1 July 1851. Gold fever gripped the town of 23,000 in the middle of that year. Upon hearing of the riches found in the Blue Mountains outside Sydney, and then in the Victorian interior, men abandoned the township to seek their fortunes. Shops and businesses were deserted. Public servants decamped to stake their claims.

Friendly societies were not left unscathed by these movements. They relied upon regular social meetings and the recurring payment of membership fees. The former cemented social bonds, while the latter ensured adequate funds to support members in hardship. As Blainey explains, the exodus left organisations like IOOF close to collapse.[9]

In 1850, Polish-born rabbi Moses Rintel was elected Provincial Grand Master, providing a steady hand during this precarious time. The odd fellows were non-denominational, so Rintel's faith was inconsequential. The order's only religious overtones were a belief in a supreme being and the moral precept to help others.

Like his Biblical namesake, Rintel was a leader of men. His name is the first featured on the IOOF honour board. His eight years as a senior leader provided both consolidation and growth. The tributes to Rintel upon his death in 1880 indicate that he was involved with many organisations throughout his life. The *Jewish Herald* said:

~

Death, 'the great leveller', has torn from our midst one of the oldest surviving landmarks of colonial Jewish history, in the person of the Rev. Moses Rintel, senior Jewish Minister of the Hebrew community of Melbourne, 'the pioneer of Judaism in this colony, and the first authorised Jewish Minister'.[10]

~

By 1858, IOOF had six lodges across Victoria: the original Duke of York Lodge; the Fitzroy Lodge; the Loyal Brothers and the Loyal Ashby lodges in Geelong; and one each in the Melbourne suburbs of Collingwood and Prahran. Lodges also operated in the colonies of Tasmania and South Australia. IOOF expanded in the following years to Ballarat, Bendigo, Colac and the Western District, and throughout Gippsland. It remained strong in these areas for at least a century. Even today, one can see the remnants of these lodges on the foundation stones and placards of halls in towns such as Walhalla and Colac.

Authorities added 'Ancient' to the start of the IOOF name in 1862 to distinguish it from the other odd fellows. IOOF's growth was steady but slow. Victorian government data collected in 1865 showed that IOOF had 22 lodges (fifth in size on a ladder of thirteen), while archrival Manchester Unity bolted ahead with 106.

IOOF's membership numbers suffered from not being affiliated with an order in the United Kingdom. British immigrants would usually renew their allegiance with their home country order, such as the Manchester Unity or Hibernians, rather than switch to another. The question of affiliation was often raised, with many members wondering if staying independent was wise. In the 1860s, an American visitor ended that isolation and initiated a new affiliation.

Founded in 1819, the American odd fellows separated from their British brothers in 1843. They had evolved their own rules and developed a Puritan-tinged strain of oddfellowship in the American north-east. There were no pub meetings for these odd fellows. The Victorian odd fellows had contacted their American brothers in 1859. After correspondence, the two parties reached an agreement. In 1862, Brother A.J. Gunnison set out across the Pacific, only for his ship, the S.S. *Golden Gate*, to sink in a fire that killed 173 people. Gunnison survived, but his mission ended.

The Civil War intervened, and the American odd fellows focused on domestic issues. The connection faded until Brother Augustus D. Meacham renewed contact with the Victorians in the mid-1860s. He travelled to Victoria as the Special Deputy Grand Sire for Australia of the Grand Lodge of the Independent Order of Odd Fellows of the United States of America. Arriving in November 1867, he undertook his tour of duty with zeal. 'It almost seems that Meacham had mesmerised the Victorians,' writes Blainey.[11]

On Saturday, 22 February 1868, the Victorian IOOF officially joined with the American odd fellows at the Geelong Town Hall. So began an affiliation that would wax and wane for the next six decades.

The American alliance was not universally popular. The United States was not yet a global superpower, and Victorians still felt far more cultural affinity with Britain. Aside from the puritanism of the American order, the Victorian odd fellows were uncomfortable with aspects like the racial segregation advocated by the Americans. The American rules stipulated that only 'free whites' could join. The Victorians opposed that policy, with local lodges counting Indian, Pacific Islanders and Chinese members. IOOF general secretary, Abraham Cohen, as Blainey recounts, provided an eloquent riposte to the Americans:

~

[Y]ou will readily perceive that the retention of the words, 'free white', places us in an unequivocal position with some of our own members, and exposes us to the calumny of a considerable portion of this community, who have always been taught to consider every man equally entitled to respect, irrespective of Country or Colour.[12]

~

Segregation was one example of why the Australian and American orders were distant cousins rather than brothers. The Australians were pragmatists. The Americans espoused more imperial notions. As Meacham put it, they aimed to add 'more links to that great chain of Universal Brotherhood, which we believe is destined to encircle the earth.'[13] The American link was frivolous to many members. The Victorian lodges put their faith in skilfully managing member funds and providing practical services as the surest way to keep members happy.

While IOOF had dallied with the United States, the birth in 1871 of another friendly society—the Australian Natives' Association (ANA)—reflected an emerging sense of patriotism in the colonies. The ANA was staunchly nationalist. In contrast, IOOF was apolitical. By the century's end, the ANA's outspoken stance on political issues won it three times as many members in Victoria as IOOF.

Friendly societies surged in popularity during the second half of the 1800s. However, their regulatory framework was scant. Sporadically, governments imposed piecemeal reforms on the sector. Most of this legislative scaffolding originated from Britain and trickled into the Australian colonies. The UK parliament enacted the *Friendly Societies Act* (1793) as part of reforms to Britain's 'poor laws'. At the time, the act made friendly societies the only type of association in

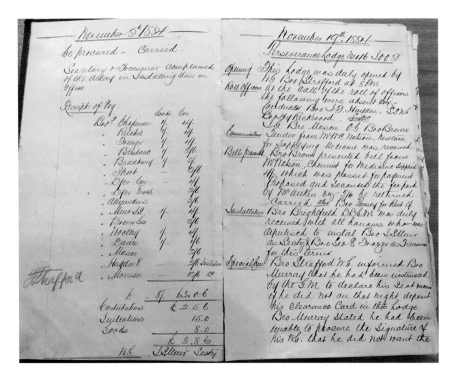

An old IOOF ledger. Good recordkeeping was essential for the financial health of lodges and orders. Insignia Financial

which it was legal for labourers to meet freely. The act was revised continuously over the next century.

Governments at the time had little wish to provide social welfare. And friendly societies did not want governments meddling in their affairs. An uneasy truce ensued. Summarising, Blainey writes in his history of Australia, *A Land Half Won*: 'Initiative, thrift, and self-help with a dash of luck were widely extolled as virtues. The idea that the government should often intervene was not widely held. Most people believed that by their own efforts—as small owners or as wage earners—they could make a living and keep self-respect.'[14]

In *Mutual Aid or Welfare State: Australia's Friendly Societies*, Green and Cromwell touch upon the spirit of self-reliance that inspired societies like IOOF: 'The desire for independence was the foundation stone of friendly society services.'[15]

~

Higher membership numbers, more stringent oversight from authorities, and the gradual incorporation of actuarial methodologies meant pub rules no longer sufficed. Friendly societies increasingly had to justify themselves to authorities like the Registrar of Friendly Societies. They gradually professionalised to meet these new challenges.[16]

~

Skilled funds management became more crucial for friendly societies. Members held leaders accountable for any squandering of funds. Poor handling of sick pay or funeral benefits could quickly undo a lodge. In his IOOF history, Blainey writes: 'While the regalia, ceremony, and passwords caught the imagination, it was money that held a lodge together.'[17]

Melbourne had prospered from the Gold Rush, but life was still a struggle for the average working person, which included most IOOF members. Influenza, typhoid, smallpox and other infectious diseases regularly brought severe illness, disability and death to the community throughout the second half of the 1800s. Work accidents also took their toll on the population. As Blainey notes, life expectancy was shorter in that age, and becoming a member of a friendly society meant 'some security during months of adversity'.[18]

In 1871, the organisation's longer-term security was on leaders' minds when planning for a city head office. The proliferation of lodges in the inner suburbs partly drove the decision. IOOF lobbied for a free government land grant on Russell Street, opposite the town's main gaol. (One of the IOOF members involved in securing the land was David Gaunson, who would be a counsel on the bushranger Ned Kelly's legal defence team.)

The Most Worthy Grand Master Brother Kidston laid the foundation stone for the new Russell Street Hall on 20 August 1872. Although some—especially those from country lodges—had reservations about its cost, the hall served as a meeting place for suburban lodges. It was hired out by other groups, providing an immediate income stream. A new building was erected on the site in 1887 to accommodate the organisation's growth. The building was dedicated to the IOOF motto: 'Friendship, Love and Truth'.

In 1876, the Victorian Royal Commission on Friendly Societies imposed further restraints and conditions on their operations.

It forced friendly societies to provide detailed financial data, forming the basis of ongoing five-year forecasts. The increased regulation meant more work for the mainly volunteer-run organisations. The Royal Commission also floated the idea of introducing government sickness insurance, before performing a U-turn and concluding that 'no scheme could be devised' which did not 'carry with it something of the appearance of a relief system'. The Royal Commission reported that it had found Australian working men, even more than those in England, to be implacably opposed to any such plan.'[19]

Tension was also developing between the financial aims of the organisation and its social and ceremonial functions. Some members viewed the social elements as essential and, quite simply, fun. Others took a more economical view, questioning what they saw as frivolous spending on banners, honour boards and ceremonial garb. The arguments over expenditure exposed the paradoxical strength and weakness of societies like IOOF: without social bonds, financial cooperation was difficult to procure, and without a sound financial footing, social bonds were hard to establish.

IOOF's membership numbers significantly accelerated during the 1870s and 1880s, rising from around 2000 in 1873 to more than 5000 by 1882. It still lagged behind the numbers of some larger orders, but it remained an assured presence, impressing with its sober management rather than political rhetoric (like the ANA) or opulent displays of success (like Manchester Unity). Leaders such as Abraham Cohen, Frederick Batcheldor, William Stirling, John Fraser, Henry Vine and Michael Kidston did their part, assiduously managing IOOF through various travails.

But the good times did not last forever, and Melbourne's four decades of growth ended in the 1890s. Rising land and asset prices had snowballed into a speculative bubble buoyed by British investors looking for high-growth returns from the colonies. 'The land boom and bust and the horrifying trail of bad and unserviceable debt made the slump much worse than it might otherwise have been. Victoria was by far the worst hit Australasian colony,' writes Robert Murray in *150 Years of Spring Street: The Victorian Government 1850s to 21st Century*.[20]

Between 1890 and 1895, Melbourne's unemployment rate jumped from 5 per cent to 30 per cent. The economic historian (and, from 1892 to 1905, friendly societies registrar) Sir Timothy Augustine Coghlan summarised:

~

The distress in Melbourne at the middle of June 1892 was tragic, and The Argus newspaper, a not too friendly observer of the unemployed, stated that at least 2000 people were on the verge of starvation; others quite as well qualified to judge considered that twice that number would be nearer the reality.[21]

~

In *Marvellous Melbourne: The Emergence of an Australian City*, historian Jill Roe outlines the procession towards panic in a scenario that would be repeated in Victoria almost a century later:

~

First, many building societies went bankrupt. Then, as ordinary people realised that they might be left in the lurch, there was a run on the Melbourne branches of the banks. People rushed to withdraw their money. In that rush, which began in 1889 but was not serious until 1892, local banks collapsed. In 1893, by Government order, all banks were closed for a week. The move had been from uncertainty to panic.[22]

~

IOOF was not immune from this spiral. Balancing social bonds and financial demands was challenging. Individual lodges decided on the payment of sickness funds to individuals and how long they could carry an unfinancial member. Brotherhood fostered loyalty and trust, but a lodge still had to balance its books. Unfinancial members became a burden. By the end of 1893, one in every six members could no longer afford their fees, rendering them technically ineligible for help when they needed it most. Lodge funds were depleted as they tried to cover the costs of those fallen upon hard times.

Even the Duke of York Lodge was in trouble. It lost a substantial amount on a Richmond property investment, but managed to scrape through the decade.

The economic woes of the 1890s were lightened by a renewed focus on social activities, with the formation of an odd fellows' cricket league in the mid-1890s, the launch of a brass band and the establishment of women's lodges and junior lodges for boys. The women's lodges were based on the American odd fellows' Rebekah lodges. Blainey writes: 'A friendly society that believed in caring for the sick and the dying, at last, realised that women usually did these tasks more skilfully than men.'[23]

These initiatives were bright spots when the society was unsure it would celebrate its 50th birthday. The remainder of the 1890s saw IOOF and its lodges count their losses and hope for better times in the new century. Reflecting on its struggles, Grand Master Brother Walter M. Gamble said, 'A crumb or two of comfort is all that had fallen to my lot.'[24] IOOF had been sorely tested but held firm to its ideal of friendship, love and truth.

Santa Claus and children at an IOOF Christmas party in Bexley, Sydney, in 1934. Families gathered at lodges to enjoy each other's company. Ted Hood, Mitchell Library, State Library of New South Wales

CHAPTER 4

WARS, DEPRESSION
AND UNCERTAINTY

Could a lodge member have a second wife's funeral expenses covered if he had already accessed funding for his first wife's funeral? 'The Grand Master's answer was that he could not,' the *Ballarat Star* reported on 14 March 1902. 'Br. [Brother] Martin moved, and Br. Crowen seconded that the answer be disagreed with. The Grand Secretary strenuously supported the decision, which, on being put to the meeting, was upheld.'[1]

The bread-and-butter issues for friendly societies, which made a real difference in members' lives, often came down to vigorous debates between lodge secretaries and the grandees at the head office. These debates often focused on fulfilling members' financial needs to provide them and their families with the dignity and respect they deserved, balanced by ensuring the organisation held sufficient funds to stay solvent. This tension was at the heart of friendly societies. IOOF's officials had to frequently make difficult decisions while keeping members happy.

The popularity of friendly societies made sense in the 1800s. They were a grassroots response to the fundamental challenges to financial security and economic wellbeing at the time. Alongside churches, charities and other philanthropic concerns, they were among the primary providers of financial relief for middle-class and working-class people. They provided a communal and trusted setting for pooling significant sums of money, which they often invested in growing wealth for their members, usually in property, private business investments (sometimes owned or recommended by members) or bank deposits. Friendly societies were among the earliest non-bank financial institutions and might even be called funds managers.

After Australia's federation in 1901, the new national government set about uniting the colonies. In the early 1900s, the Commonwealth government introduced significant social welfare reforms. Following state-based schemes, it introduced old-age pensions in 1908 and invalid pensions in 1910. IOOF had initiated member-funded pension schemes only a decade before, but the economic downturn of the 1890s had extinguished them.

The new government initiatives did not initially impact friendly societies significantly and were aimed at the destitute and entrenched poor. By contrast, friendly society membership was drawn mainly from the skilled working class, small-business owners and middle-class wage earners. The societies supported many of these welfare initiatives. The experiences of the 1890s had made many members far more empathetic to the plight of people experiencing poverty.

Governments were now starting to encroach on the friendly societies' domain. Another significant move towards more government intervention in social welfare came with the *War Pensions Act* (1914) and the *Australian Soldiers' Repatriation Act* (1917), commonly known as 'repat'. These pieces of legislation enabled the Commonwealth bureaucracy to develop its welfare provision capabilities and sow the seeds for a more comprehensive social security system.

One of the original purposes for friendly societies was to protect ordinary people against the financial enfeeblement that could arise from an illness. Infectious diseases were rampant. Workplace accidents were also widespread and often fatal. Illness or injury could be a slippery slope into poverty. In *Mutual Aid or Welfare State: Australia's Friendly Societies*, Green and Cromwell write:

~

In colonial Australia, illness and accidents were feared perhaps more than death. When the wage earner fell ill or was injured, the loss of earnings alone could have calamitous results. And it could mean doctors' bills to pay, perhaps by going into debt. The solution was mutual aid.[2]

~

Friendly societies enabled ordinary working people to access affordable and dignified medical care in the days before universal health coverage. In addition to paying out benefits, many societies also contracted an on-call doctor for members and their families. These doctors maintained their private practice while also serving lodge members. In addition, they verified members' health status and vetted the health of new members. The lodge doctor scheme also incentivised doctors to service rural areas by providing them with a guaranteed pool of patients and income.

The 1890s depression had put extra strain on the relationship between doctors and lodges. As is commonly the case, economic downturns can seriously impact people's health and the medical system. However, the scheme generally worked well: members received discounted services, and doctors enjoyed a steady income. The service was also a selling point for attracting new members.

A dole queue at a wharf in Circular Quay, Sydney, June 1931. Friendly society membership provided financial security for many Australians. *The Sydney Morning Herald*

However, the alliance between doctors and societies wasn't always untroubled. The scheme demanded much time and energy from predominantly volunteer-run organisations like IOOF. Indeed, the financial arrangements between the societies and doctors were a point of simmering conflict for decades. The British Medical Association (BMA)—which also represented Australian doctors until 1962—was a persistent sparring partner. Doctors complained they didn't get paid enough to deal with members' demands and the nitpicking of the lodges' bean counters. Members, meanwhile, complained that doctors treated them like second-class patients.

In the early 1900s, around one-third of Victorians accessed medical care through friendly societies, and a little over 40 per cent of Victorian doctors were contracted by the societies. David Green writes that the BMA 'was complaining bitterly that the profession was being "sweated" by the [society] medical clubs, which were then widespread, so widespread that in 1892 the president of the Medical

Society of Victoria warned that a state of "club socialism" was fast approaching.'[3]

Tensions came to a head in 1918, when doctors went on strike against the friendly societies. The doctors were arguing that the societies remunerated them poorly, and did not means-test members joining the scheme. Members would receive the same medical coverage regardless of high or low income. The doctors felt this denied them access to higher-income private fee-paying patients because these patients opted to join the society medical clubs. But the friendly societies viewed equal access for all members as intrinsic to their ethos and opposed implementing a means test.

The doctors' industrial action persisted for three years. The societies even looked to import British doctors to circumvent the strike at one stage. Eventually, the societies conceded to the BMA on most points. Power shifted to the medical profession. Green sums up: 'Henceforth, medical care was to be a producer-dominated market. And when, in later years, governments attempted to collectivise medical care, the doctors were sufficiently powerful to insist the collectivisation took place on their terms.'[4]

A small but significant aspect of friendly societies' power was diminished. The doctors' strike was a harbinger of the disruption the next few decades would bring, as the power of the societies in this area gradually declined.

Meanwhile, a global conflict of even greater importance had begun. World War I started in 1914 and soon embroiled Australian troops. The war quickly dented the societies' coffers and hit membership numbers.

'Enlistments were soon so brisk that the official records of the lodge could not keep up with them,' writes Blainey. 'Ultimately, enlistments in Victoria were on such a scale that the Grand Lodge spent heavily—£6000 in the first three years—meeting the annual lodge fees of the enlisted men.'[5]

Like the rest of the nation, the tragedy of war touched IOOF, which commemorated the tragedy with an honour board containing the names of all 230 members who had died during the war serving the country.

Following the end of the war, the influenza pandemic then hit hard, further straining resources. Blainey writes: 'At the Odd Fellows' hall in Melbourne the pleas for help from individual lodges read like the chronicle of a medieval plague.'[6]

An article titled 'The Influenza Handicap' in Sydney's *Daily Telegraph* reported that the NSW IOOF abandoned its 1919 annual meeting because of the pandemic. The report also relayed that the Grand Master told the meeting that the 'strictest economy had been observed in connection with the management fund, with the result that the deficiency had been further decreased . . . Notwithstanding the huge payments made by the order in connection with the influenza outbreak.'[7]

The war and the pandemic left the friendly societies weakened financially and at a crossroads socially. A cautious outlook for the national economy also dampened their hopes that they might replenish their coffers anytime soon. People were saving their pennies and cutting their spending. It was a testing time for IOOF.

After the war, the theatricality of fraternal orders and their passwords, ceremonies and regalia perhaps held less appeal. The Returned & Services League of Australia (RSL) was formed in 1916, and within three years it had 114,700 members. The RSL attracted men in the same age bracket as the recruitment targets for societies like IOOF. Undoubtedly, the mateship of war bonded these men in a way that friendly societies could not. Blaney writes: 'The Order was too theatrical, too secret, too ritualistic in its ceremonies to appeal to younger Australians of the 1920s.'[8]

It was not only the RSL that started attracting the increased patronage of Australians. As well as competing with fellow societies, IOOF contended with a new array of civic and volunteer organisations. Legacy, Rotary Australia, the Country Women's Association, the Boy Scouts and the Girl Guides, and Surf Life Saving Australia were all established between 1900 and 1930. Sporting competitions, including suburban and country football leagues, also boomed. Social options were bountiful. Friendly societies could still offer financial security, but the social element was under threat. Initiatives like IOOF's women's and juvenile lodges helped broaden the society's appeal, but societies struggled to keep pace.

Emerging from a troubled period, young people embraced modernity, hoping that technological advances and more liberal attitudes might help them leave behind the pain. The social mores of Australians were changing, and the societies started to look stuffy. 'In Australian towns and suburbs in the 1920s, the lodge was not the favourite venue for fraternity and mateship,' writes Blaney.[9]

By 1928, IOOF in Victoria was still well behind the membership numbers of other societies. The leading organisations at this time were the Australian Natives' Association (33,200 members); Manchester Unity (26,600); the Rechabites (16,000); the Druids (13,000); the Foresters (9200); and IOOF (8400 members). IOOF had made slight gains in other states, but interstate connections, usually mediated by the Australasian Grand Lodge (which met intermittently), still lagged. Without the UK connection of Manchester Unity or the patriotic aura of the ANA, IOOF continued to sell itself mainly on its funds-handling abilities.

During this period, IOOF proudly called itself the 'biggest friendly society in the world', pointing to its international member-ship numbers of around 1.2 million. Of course, these numbers included the massive IOOF membership base in the United States. While those US-boosted numbers sounded impressive, IOOF was strictly a middleweight in Australia. Its main attraction to members was its solid track record of financial management.

Enthusiasm for the connection to the American odd fellows was also waning. In the 1870s and 1880s, the Victorian Grand Lodge and

Miners in the early 20th century in the Victorian town of Walhalla, which was the location of a longstanding IOOF lodge. The town's IOOF hall was destroyed by fire in December 1951. Museums Victoria

its leaders, influenced by the teetotalling Americans, had encouraged lodges to shift their meetings away from pubs, and, if possible, to purchase or build their own halls. Lodges usually benefited financially from owning property by hiring facilities for local groups and social functions.

By the early 1920s, the Victorian odd fellows had moved away from the more Puritan American strain of oddfellowship, not exactly reverting to the freewheeling attitudes of the 1840s pioneers but embracing a more relaxed approach. Many, including the Grand Secretary for Victoria, Brother C.E. Wilson, viewed the initiations and ceremonies borrowed from the American odd fellows as archaic, pompous and a waste of time: 'The use of ceremony and symbol does not of itself appeal to the average member of our reserved and undemonstrative race.'[10]

Calls for a formal split from the Americans grew in the 1920s, as Australians became more patriotic. In 1927, a report by a former Victorian Grand Master, Walter Selwood, recommended IOOF bid farewell to the Americans: 'The time is ripe for the IOOF in Australia to be established on an Australian basis in all things.'[11] The feeling was that the American link weakened the patriotic standing of IOOF, a salient factor following World War I. Selwood likely had an eye on the ANA's patriotic outlook.

Selwood's recommendations were not acted upon until the October 1929 Victorian Grand Lodge annual meeting, when a motion was raised to split from the Americans. The vote supported the split, 63 to 43, but it was not a large enough majority to put the issue to bed. Influential lodges, including Colac, voted against the break principally because it risked the unity of the Australian Independent Order of Odd Fellows—the other state bodies were sticking with the Americans. Victoria was the only one to secede, discarding the old American-derived rituals and admitting women for the first time to branches or subordinate lodges. Blainey writes:

~

The secret passwords were no more. The initiation ceremony became brisk. The old beards and gowns went to the tip or were seen only at fancy dress balls.[12]

~

The split was perhaps of less interest to rank-and-file members than to the noble grands, as this report in the *Shepparton Advertiser* highlights:

~

The quarterly meeting of the Shepparton Independent Order of Oddfellows was held in the lodgeroom at the rear of the Star theatre on Monday evening last. There was a good attendance. The chair was occupied by the N.G., Bro. R.A. Strawhorn. Accounts totalling £50 were passed for payment . . . A letter was also received from the Grand Lodge of Victoria stating that they were severing their connection with the Sovereign Grand Lodge of America.—Received. Games concluded a very enjoyable evening.[13]

~

Some Victorian lodges remained loyal to the Americans. Three years later, there was an unsuccessful push for reunification with the Americans, and—more crucially—with their interstate brothers. The schism was less about America than about the severing of ties with the rest of the state-based Australian lodges.

This office cabinet from Insignia Financial's collection dates from the late 19th century.
Insignia Financial

Along with the split, October 1929 also marked the beginning of what became known as the Great Depression. The Wall Street stock market crash ushered in years of economic hardship. Replicating the pattern of the 1890s, many friendly society members held tight to their hard-earned benefits for as long as possible. As conditions worsened, more members dropped out, giving up any claim to benefits in the future. Australians confronted some of the harshest economic conditions the country had ever faced. Suddenly unemployed, many current and potential members baulked at the idea of forking out fees while they were experiencing their own financial hardships. Even if membership of an Order entailed a certain amount of insurance against financial distress, it was hard to sell the idea to those living hand to mouth as the economy worsened.

The 1929 crash was symptomatic of broader problems in the global economy, and it sparked a worldwide economic downturn. The Australian economy experienced falling commodity prices and greater competition from other countries. Australia also borrowed vast sums from UK banks and investors, but as the economy slowed access to these funds slowed to a trickle. Unemployment peaked at 32 per cent in 1932. It would take Australia almost a decade to recover—only for another tragic episode to unfold in 1939 with the beginning of World War II.

During the 1930s, a new economic orthodoxy took root. British economist John Maynard Keynes advocated a more active role in the economy for governments struggling to control unemployment. Just as Adam Smith's ideas in the 1700s shaped the global economy for two centuries, Keynesianism fundamentally shifted government policies and the economy. The call for government interventions dovetailed with an expansion of social welfare programs.

These ideas soon influenced the policies of the Australian federal government, affecting friendly societies, including the Odd Fellows.[14] Labor governments introduced child endowment in 1941; a pension for widows in 1942; an allowance for wives in 1943; additional appropriations for the children of pensioners in 1943; and unemployment, sickness and special benefits in 1945. Blainey writes: 'The old world in which friendly societies were the main providers of emergency help was about to vanish. Nothing could permanently prop up that world.'[15]

The nature of societies like IOOF changed drastically during the first half of the 20th century: Federation, World War I, the influenza pandemic, the Great Depression and then World War II drove those changes. Fresh ideas in economics and culture also played a part. During these tumultuous times, IOOF had to answer some tough questions. Where did it fit in the economic landscape? What was its role in society? How could it best serve its members?

Friendly societies were seen by many as socially archaic. Their economic viability was also under threat. The social and financial bonds that once tied members to the societies were being undone. IOOF had to rethink its purpose and mission to survive in the post–World War II era.

The finance and insurance industries began to modernise in the postwar economic boom period. Friendly societies had to follow suit. Max Dupain, Mitchell Library, State Library of New South Wales

CHAPTER 5

LIVING WITH THE WELFARE STATE

✳

For the Victorian IOOF, even into the 1940s, reunification with the Australasian Grand Lodge and the American odd fellows remained an issue. It was back on the agenda in October 1941 when Brother Reuben Rosengarten argued that the Victorian IOOF could better participate in the rollout of federal welfare schemes by reuniting with the national lodge. Rosengarten's proposal was defeated, 66 to 46.

In October 1943, the Victorian Grand Lodge voted again on reunification, and this time the motion was carried. But wartime travel restrictions and society by-laws meant it took until 8 August 1944 for the Australasian Grand Lodge to approve reaffiliation. The Victorian Grand Lodge took another vote only two months later. This time, 65 to 57 votes overturned the reunification. Victoria once again walked alone. In October 1945, unity forces raised the motion again, but it was voted down, with the supplement that the Victorian Grand Lodge would not revisit the issue for five years.

Meanwhile, the broader picture for IOOF and other friendly societies involved politics and the economy. Post-war reforms to the Australian economy created long-term shifts in the public's expectations about the state's role in their lives.

The relationship between government—at both the state and federal levels—and friendly societies has constantly evolved. The societies initially emerged in the transition from the pre-modern to a market-based economy when the government's role was limited. But two world wars and a crippling economic depression brought forth more strident calls for state interventions. The popular belief grew that the state should offer basic welfare, at least for those who could not provide for themselves.

In retrospect, the expansion of social security was a case of the friendly societies moving aside as big government was moving in. Politicians and economists would debate for decades the merits of this intervention. Indeed, the debate remains relevant even today.

Driven by Keynesian ideas, both the conservative and labour sides of politics reached a consensus that the government had a role in the economy and, where possible, should help those in need. But how far should it intervene? For friendly societies, predicting how this would affect them was impossible. In hindsight, the effects were profound.

In *Australia's Welfare Wars*, Philip Mendes outlines the social welfare reforms of the 1940s that reshaped the relationship between the government, Australians and the economy over the next four decades. He cites the Joint Parliamentary Committee on Social Security, set up initially by Prime Minister Robert Menzies' United Australia Party government in 1941, as a critical turning point:

~

The Committee's First Interim Report reported that . . . 'a considerable proportion of Australia's citizens are poorly housed, ill-clothed or ill-nourished—living in conditions which reflect no credit on a country such as ours'. The Report recommended that social services would contribute to the the war effort 'by improving the morale and willingness to work of the employees, who will feel that a regime which is prepared, even at this time of emergency, to improve their conditions is worth working and fighting for.'[1]

~

The reforms aimed to address market inadequacies in alleviating financial distress and poverty. The measures introduced included child endowment, funeral benefits for deceased pensioners, new maternity allowances, widows' pensions, unemployment, sickness and pharmaceutical benefits, and hospital and tuberculosis benefits. These reforms encroached upon the offerings of the friendly societies. Members were left asking: why pay into a friendly society if the government will provide the same benefits?

Even Menzies, a paragon of conservative values, played his role in creating the Australian welfare state. What Menzies introduced in 1941 was soon expanded by the successive federal Labor governments of John Curtin and Ben Chifley. Even when Menzies returned to the prime ministership in 1949 as the leader of the Liberal–Country coalition, he did not roll back these welfare measures despite Australia having left the war years behind. Instead, Menzies and successive Coalition governments added programs throughout the 1950s and 1960s.

The decline of friendly societies was becoming apparent even in the 1940s. Calls for members to get involved were common, as in this report from 27 May 1940 about an IOOF lodge meeting in the *Shepparton Advertiser*:

~

The social committee reported that, owing to the lack of support given them by members, they were reluctant to carry on. After many members had expressed their appreciation of the work done by the committee, it was resolved to invite the members' wives and lady friends to the next meeting with a view to forming a ladies' committee to help with the lodge social activities.[2]

~

Medical and pharmaceutical benefits continued to be a necessary part of the friendly society business. The societies still held some collective clout in these areas, primarily through the dispensaries the societies often operated in partnerships.

In 1946, the friendly societies sought to widen their rights in an area where they had banded together to form pharmacy dispensaries to service their members. The friendly societies had had success in this endeavour since the late 1800s, sometimes in conflict with the Pharmacy Guild of Australia.

Friendly society–run pharmacy dispensaries, like this one in Charters Towers, Queensland, photographed in 1909, provided access to medicines for many working-class people. State Library of Queensland

According to the Government Statist, 34 friendly society dispensaries were registered in Victoria at the time, servicing about 500,000 members. Defending the friendlies in this dispute, Williamstown state MP John Lemmon said:

~

There is no justification for the fear that friendly societies will do anything other than to seek to maintain their present position and to render valuable service to the rank and file of the community, which has been the principle characteristic of the movement for the last 75 years.[3]

~

The societies continued the fight, but it became increasingly difficult as the political terrain shifted beneath their feet and members deserted. Many new federal benefits had eaten into the financial appeal of membership. Though targeted to the lowest-income earners, initiatives like funeral, unemployment and pharmaceutical benefits dissuaded many from joining societies.

The IOOF 100th grand session was held at the Russell Street headquarters in 1958. James Meneilly was elected IOOF Grand Master at this session, the youngest Grand Master in IOOF history. He served again as Grand Master in 1974. Courtesy of Chris Meneilly

A letter to *The Age* newspaper in 1948 from Mr Marion Robertson of St Kilda East summed up the challenge: 'Friendly society delegates would do well to concentrate on demanding from their boards and officials the reforms by way of modernised benefits that are a long outstanding need.'[4]

Most lodges continued in reasonable financial health, but ageing and dying members needed to be more readily replaced. The once-thriving cricket teams and brass bands of the early 1900s, which attracted social members, were disappearing. Friendly societies were becoming relics of a bygone age. The radical disruptions of the past half-century had created an existential crisis for the friendly society movement.

The decline was happening elsewhere, too. In the United Kingdom, the introduction of the *National Insurance Act* and the National Health Scheme hollowed out many friendly societies. 'The crucial question for the 1950s,' Blainey writes, 'was whether the societies would view the change as an opportunity or an obstacle.'[5]

Friendly societies were not big businesses. Still largely member-run volunteer organisations with a skeleton staff of remunerated office bearers, they lacked highly trained executives and experienced boards. Organisations like IOOF mostly had to react on the run. It didn't have the ear of politicians, like the ANA did, nor the numerical clout of Manchester Unity. It did, however, have a knack for survival and an ethos of putting its members first.

In July 1953, the Menzies government introduced the medical benefits scheme, a rudimentary precursor to Medibank and Medicare that provided modest pharmaceutical and hospital cover for low-income earners and pensioners. Friendly societies administered and distributed some of these benefits to members.

The scheme required people to join registered societies to access benefits. But the federal government stipulated that those joining did not have to become initiated members, which created a two-tiered membership structure. Active members resented that others could become members without buying into the organisation's ongoing financial and social health or its broader ethos of friendship, love and truth.

By 1963, around 8000 of IOOF's 20,000 members were 'group' members, using IOOF to access their government-sponsored benefits. Acting as welfare dispensaries kept the societies alive as they received government compensation for providing these services, but it also

The Whitlam Government initiated healthcare reforms, including Medibank, that changed Australian society.
Graeme Fletcher/Newspix

weakened their ethos, which was to encourage financial independence and self-empowerment.

The decline did not happen overnight and there were still bright spots throughout the 1950s and 1960s. Reports showed several new lodges had opened in Melbourne's growing south-eastern suburbs. From the 1 April 1953 issue of the *Dandenong Journal*:

~

A new branch of the IOOF Lodge was formed at Dandenong on March 17th and sets out with an encouraging membership of 30 . . . Grand Master Brother E.J. McMillan addressed the Lodge, also explaining the benefits of the Government's new medical scheme . . . The new Noble Grand proposed the toast to 'Our Queen', which was musically honored.[6]

~

A 'lodge report' in the 24 September 1954 issue of the *Williamstown Chronicle* indicated that IOOF was still thriving in Melbourne's west:

On Monday, 13th, a large number attended a very successful meeting in the Ramsay Memorial Hall. After the meeting competitive bowls were played against Loyal Gordon (Newport) and Loyal Yarraville. Both visiting teams were beaten by 1 point. On Monday last all lodges on this side of Footscray attended the Loyal Gordon lodgeroom on the occasion of the visit of the Grand Master, Bro R. Rosengarten and members of Grand Lodge executive. Reports indicate that the IOOF is numerically growing and is financially very secure.[7]

However, the general trend was worrying. Across Australia, friendly society membership declined by a third between 1948 and 1962. The better-established societies, such as IOOF, Manchester Unity, the ANA and the United Ancient Order of Druids, were helped by being registered to administer health benefits. Those without such a licence struggled to stay afloat. Many disbanded or merged with the more prominent societies. Life offices like AMP and National Mutual also squeezed the societies in areas such as work-related insurance, with employers often opting for these policies.

In 1964, IOOF opened a new office named Mackay House in the Melbourne central business district (CBD) at the cost of £252,000. It acquired good income from leasing three floors to Commonwealth agencies, including the Bureau of Meteorology. Centralised administration continued apace as the head office assumed tasks once handled by the lodges, many of which were now struggling to maintain their operations.

By 1967, some 95 lodges remained across Victoria, but many were almost defunct. Lodges disappeared as the number of ageing members exceeded new recruits. The remaining lodges merged and rationalised. A few more vital lodges, including Williamstown's Loyal Philanthropic Lodge in Melbourne's west and several country lodges in western Victoria, including the Loyal Lowan, Loyal Budjik, Loyal Wimmera and Loyal Grampians, continued to foster lodge social life while maintaining sound financials and advancing some commercial development.

By the early 1970s, IOOF's financials felt the effect of replacement by welfare state provision and competition from life insurance offices and more prominent societies. The 1972 election of Gough Whitlam's federal Labor government was a watershed moment in Australian history and presented further challenges to friendly societies. After its euphoric win, Labor changed the Commonwealth's medical insurance and social welfare programs. The most significant reform was the introduction of Medibank, which greatly expanded the Coalition's medical benefits scheme, introduced in 1953.

Medibank started operating on 1 October 1975. Along with other societies, IOOF became a Medibank agent, receiving claims and paying them out on behalf of the Commonwealth while receiving enough from the government to cover costs without making a profit. IOOF adapted its offerings and created a Dental Benefit Fund and a Mediplan scheme, which took up where Medibank left off with coverage for ancillary medical services.

The Fraser government ended Medibank's monopoly in 1976, giving the friendly societies room to manoeuvre. But IOOF had already ceded ground to the ANA and HBA, and many who might have considered an IOOF health fund were now content with Medibank. In its advertising for health funds in 1977, IOOF offered 'bigger, better and faster benefits'. However, such offerings did little to boost its coffers, as the profit margins were slim.

IOOF explored other opportunities in the mid-1970s, chiefly life insurance policies, but these schemes were a mild success at best. The IOOF hierarchy was running out of ideas and low on funds. The society side was losing money and the social side was virtually extinct. The society was out of touch, adrift and demographically challenged. The 1975 annual report noted: 'It was a sad fact that with the passage of time more and more of the beloved members of the Order were answering the final call.'

IOOF sponsored the struggling Fitzroy Football Club in 1977 as part of a marketing effort to push its health funds and boost its profile. The campaign highlighted IOOF's proud history: 'Trust your practitioner with your health, trust IOOF to insure it. Why trust IOOF to take care of your health insurance? Because they've been taking care of people and their health for more than 130 years.'

There was even some talk in 1978 of the friendly societies creating an amalgamated health fund to challenge HBA and Medibank Private. Eight Victorian societies banded together in 1979 to form the United Health Fund, but IOOF was not among them.

In 1978, IOOF was close to insolvency. Blainey writes: 'For the year 1977–78, the Order's assets were virtually halved by the losses made in trying to expand its way out of trouble.'[8] Victorian government officials privately raised concerns with IOOF about its finances, with the organisation's grand trustees liable to be sued if the organisation collapsed.

The crisis of 1978 was brought about by a culmination of factors: a declining membership; an inability to challenge the big health funds; a lack of additional revenue from forays into life assurance policies; and excessive spending on marketing initiatives.

The new Grand Secretary, Chris Henderson, and financial controller, Kevin Homewood, hatched a plan to keep the organisation solvent. Loyal odd fellows who assisted in the fight for survival were Sydney McGregor, Secretary of the Loyal Philanthropic Lodge at Williamstown; Harold Larwood of Loyal Carnegie and a Grand Trustee for more than twenty years; Brother Robert Smith of Loyal Yarraville Lodge and also a Grand Trustee; and Brother James Meneilly, the Grand Treasurer since 1975 and a member of the Loyal Bentleigh Lodge. Membership prices were raised to the highest limit permissible. While some feared a fee hike would lead to a further exodus, the strategy resulted in a more stable financial footing for the organisation. Enough members could see the merits of membership to vindicate the higher cost, with ten per cent opting not to renew their memberships. A crisis had been averted but the big-picture problem of attracting new members and funds remained.[9]

The post-war period saw massive cultural, economic and demographic changes, which changed the landscape for IOOF and other friendly societies. IOOF entered the 1980s in a fragile state, unsure of its long-term prospects and still facing membership decline.

The 1987 stock market crash benefited friendly societies such as IOOF in the short term, as investors moved from shares to capital-guaranteed investment vehicles like Supersaver. Anton Cermak/*The Sydney Morning Herald*

CHAPTER 6

GOOD TIMES COME CRASHING DOWN

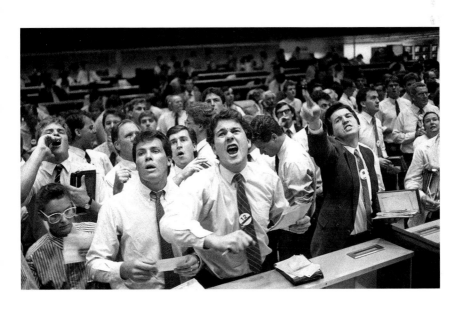

Once upon a time, the northern English county of Yorkshire was a mostly rural stretch of rolling green hills punctuated by quaint villages and a few bigger trading towns. When the steam engine revolutionised the wool industry in the 1800s, Yorkshire experienced phenomenal growth. It became an international textile manufacturing centre, making the area a hotbed for friendly societies. To meet workers' and their families' financial and social needs, fraternal orders, including the odd fellows, sprang up and prospered in towns like Sheffield, Leeds and Bradford, which together became the 'wool capital of the world'.[1]

Born near Bradford, Martyn Pickersgill became IOOF's general secretary and CEO in 1982. It was the first time a non-odd fellow assumed the top job, a historic occasion for IOOF. But even if he was not a sworn odd fellow, his Yorkshire heritage might have imbued him with a sense of the importance of the societies.

In his mid-thirties and with experience in a senior role with the ANA, Pickersgill was a breath of fresh air for IOOF. His immediate predecessor, Chris Henderson, had turned the business around following the challenging period of the late 1970s, but IOOF remained at a crossroads. The board's break with tradition was a vote of hope in the organisation's future. 'The very choice of an outsider as Chief Executive was itself a sign of the willingness of the IOOF to think of exploring new paths,' Blainey writes.[2]

Governments worldwide in the late 1970s had started turning from the Keynesian orthodoxy that had defined the post-war years towards the neoliberalism advocated by economists such as Milton Friedman. The free-market push in the United States was tagged 'Reaganomics', after the enthusiast President Ronald Reagan, and focused firmly on cuts in industry subsidies and tariffs, financial deregulation and smaller government. In the United Kingdom, led by Prime Minister Margaret Thatcher, it was 'Thatcherism'. The privatisation of many UK government enterprises influenced the thinking of Australian political leaders. Even those within the Labor Party had their heads turned by this neoliberal wave.

When Pickersgill joined in 1982, change was in the offing for the Australian economy, and friendly societies like IOOF could ill afford to dwell in the past. Regulatory and supervisory arrangements implemented following the Campbell Committee's Australian

Financial System Inquiry in 1981 ushered in a new era of competition in the financial services industry. The inquiry set the tone for the decade's economic policy and finance industry regulation. Both major parties embraced its recommendations almost in their entirety. The report begins: 'The Committee starts from the view that the most efficient way to organise economic activity is through a competitive market system which is subject to a minimum of regulation and government intervention.'[3]

The report created a blueprint for reimagining the Australian financial services industry, challenging the dominance of the big banks and enabling credit unions, building societies and friendly societies to bring much-needed choice and flexibility to consumers. The mantra at the time was consumer choice, but liberalisation also allowed financial institutions to venture beyond their traditional domains. The new regime gave smaller, non-bank financial institutions access to new markets. Still, it enabled the big players to consolidate their positions if they moved fast enough through intelligent mergers and acquisitions to create reach and scale.

Pickersgill brought ideas from his time with the ANA and had the flexibility to recognise IOOF's quirks and institutional and regulatory limits. The modest organisation had around 60 full-time staff, substantially fewer than the ANA, which had about 450. Pickersgill saw that IOOF was an organisation with a lot of potential but in need of modernisation. He quickly looked into computerising systems and processes, and administered organisational and management reforms.

More importantly, he had the strategic foresight to recognise that friendly societies would disappear unless they proved their relevance to savvy modern consumers. But how to do that? He wanted IOOF to continue its legacy of helping everyday people become financially secure—but sought new ways to do that. The past twenty years had seen a steep decline in the social elements of friendly society culture. The social and financial nexus that had bonded the societies and their members had significantly weakened. Without that social base, societies had to earn their keep commercially. More so than ever, they would have to be successful businesses first.

In August 1982, the Malcolm Fraser–led Coalition government announced plans to reduce the tax benefits enjoyed by schemes such as IOOF's popular Supersaver, which was introduced at the beginning of 1981. Supersaver was a superannuation savings-style account that promised high rates of return (anywhere from 16 to 28 per cent,

The late 1980s was a nervous time for investors. Friendly societies offered an alternative to listed investments. Neil Newitt/*The Age*

according to advertised rates) while being tax-free. Investors had to invest at least $1000 lump sum payments each year for a 10-year period to accrue the benefits of the plan. Any diminishment in the scheme's profitability would be a severe blow. Fortunately for IOOF, those plans were paused when the government announced a federal election, giving Pickersgill, general manager Kevin Homewood and the board breathing space. Formulating a strategy to offset any lessening of Supersaver's earnings was imperative.

The Supersaver fund helped keep IOOF buoyant throughout the early 1980s. The popular fund had propelled earnings for the group from $9 million in the 1980/81 financial year to $79 million the following year, and $211 million in 1982/83. Its success was crucial to IOOF and gave Pickersgill the financial strength to fund its modernisation and expansion.

On 5 March 1983, the Labor Party, led by Bob Hawke, defeated the Coalition government at a federal election. Hawke's victory followed the success of John Cain, who had led Labor to its first

Victorian election win since his father, John Cain Sr, had formed the first Labor majority government in Victoria's history in 1952. Over the next decade, the Victorian Labor government's interventions would test many businesses, including IOOF, and the banking and finance sectors.

The Hawke government soon announced that investment income earned through vehicles like Supersaver would be subject to income tax from 1 July 1984. This impending tax prompted Pickersgill and Homewood to advertise the benefits of Supersaver to retirees, especially in the seniors' magazine *Prime Time*. Despite the new tax, the board and management remained confident about Supersaver's prospects and, indeed, Supersaver continued to attract investors. The product's success leveraged IOOF's switch from health funds towards investment products. Blainey argues that the organisation's decision to 'compete vigorously with the life offices'—which he calls 'one of the most radical . . . in the long history of friendly societies in Australia'— brought lucrative rewards but higher risk.[4]

Fresh commercial opportunities would arise from the new federal government's seismic economic policy changes. The floating of the Australian dollar in late 1983 attracted international entrants to the domestic bond market, creating more volume and deeper markets. Further deregulation enabled IOOF to extend its investment products, which helped the business grow throughout the 1980s. IOOF was planting the seeds to become a significant funds manager. It was also making headway into other states. In June 1983, IOOF set up business in Queensland as the Community Benefits Association (another Odd Fellows organisation was already using the IOOF name).

The lines between the financial services sectors started to blur, leaving many businesses fretful about their place. Even the cloistered world of friendly societies felt the effect. Without their social membership base, the societies had to justify their existence in the newly deregulated marketplace.

Meanwhile, Pickersgill had identified centralisation as another essential item of business. In September 1983, a special general meeting of the Grand Lodge called a vote for lodges to cede some powers in order to streamline decision-making within the organisation. The lodges approved, sensing the necessity to surrender some of their historical rights for the broader organisation's health. The world was moving quickly, and Pickersgill and his team understood IOOF had to follow.

In the world of friendly societies, lodges and orders were always splitting, seceding and merging. Whether members were chasing a better deal elsewhere or stronger friendlies were taking over weaker ones, ceremonial oaths of loyalty sometimes took a back seat to financial considerations. Regulatory authorities also had a stake in the sector's health and occasionally convinced stronger societies to save ailing ones.

One such takeover occurred in November 1983, when the Victorian government tapped IOOF to help bail out the Hibernian Australasian Catholic Benefit Society. Founded in 1868, the Hibernians, like many other friendly societies, hit turbulent times in the late 1970s. The recession put paid to newer initiatives such as selling life insurance, leaving the venerable Hibs close to permanent hibernation. Blainey writes:

~

At Noah's Hotel, at the annual conference in November 1983, the Grand Master prepared to conduct a short ceremony of initiation that would have astonished his predecessors. In effect, the IOOF was initiating the Hibernian leaders and, thereby, their thousands of members . . . they were initiated with the simple words: 'Visitors, in friendship, love and truth, we welcome you.'[5]

~

Pickersgill applied a balanced approach to advancing IOOF. He adhered to the fiscal rectitude that members expected and reiterated the communitarian aspects of friendlies that were important to older members. Still, he and the board carefully broke new ground, diversifying the organisation to keep it relevant and profitable. An example was the Cumberland View retirement village, which opened in the south-eastern Melbourne suburb of Wheelers Hill and accommodated around 400 residents. The dream of opening a retirement home harked back to the late 1800s, and its realisation in March 1984 was a significant achievement. It also seemed a wise business move. The American trend of retirement villages had filtered through to Australia, and the arguments for their success were compelling.

By the mid-1980s, the Hawke government's superannuation initiatives encouraged people to think about where they invested their money and the retirement they could afford. Advertising taglines like 'If Johnny O'Keefe seems like only yesterday, then you better get IOOF superannuation, now' were pitched squarely at Baby Boomers thinking of retirement. Media coverage predicting the end of the old-age pension also put many on edge. Supersaver flourished in this environment, tapping into people's desire to retire comfortably.

The societies' traditional services were morphing into more sophisticated offerings. Fixed-price funeral plans, a staple since the earliest days, were still offered in partnership with funeral homes like Tobin Brothers. But IOOF started moving into building society services, retirement homes, executor and trustee services, and even a travel agency. Financial planning was becoming part of the mix too. Friendly societies were becoming a one-stop shop for mum-and-dad investors and retirees. Members could access investments, savings, home loans, insurance, travel, retirement and aged-care services in one place. The investments division increasingly subsidised many of IOOF's other business areas.

Federal Treasurer Paul Keating (left) at a press conference in December 1983 announcing the float of the dollar, with the RBA Governor Bob Johnston (right) looking on. *The Sydney Morning Herald*

In 1985, the Commonwealth awarded fifteen new banking licences, introducing competition for the big Australian trading banks and resulting in a proliferation of new securities markets. The securitisation of traditional bank assets provided IOOF with new fixed-interest securities, a staple investment vehicle for the societies. Subsequently, the managed investment bonds offered by IOOF were among Australia's most attractive investment choices.

By 1986, IOOF had $705 million in funds under management. Alongside consumer uptake, the IOOF investment team started to garner industry plaudits. Headed by former Chase-AMP executives Tony Hodges and Peter Twigg, *Executive News* magazine featured the IOOF investments team in its February–March 1986 issue. IOOF was earning a reputation as a skilled funds manager.

Proof of the investment team's acumen came when IOOF was the only friendly society fund group to produce an increased bonus rate for 1986/87, when all other comparable funds declined. Its growing success meant that in 1986, IOOF could 'white label' Supersaver as the BT Bond for the Bankers Trust Funds Management Group. The BT Bond penetrated the NSW market and grew to $600 million plus, making it one of the country's most successful white-labelled financial products, a unique success for a friendly society product.

Writing in the November 1986 *IOOF Update* newsletter, Pickersgill said:

~

Your Society is growing at a great rate. Accompanying that growth is an ever-widening spread of services designed to meet your needs. And, of course, the long-standing friendly society philosophy of self-help through mutual co-operation without the profit motive in mind, is still intact.[6]

~

The balancing act between profit and friendly society ideals continued throughout the mid-1980s. In an age rife with privatisation and rationalisation, there was an urgent sense that every organisation had to prove its worth. Consumers were actively shopping for the best deal, and financial institutions became more aggressive in marketing. At the same time, consumers still wanted the security from their friendly society investments to which they were accustomed.

IOOF still held social events, but these had moved on from the old-style meetings and social mixers. The ceremonies, regalia and secret passwords had been consigned to history, or at least to a storeroom out the back of the Russell Street head office. Echoes of the old lodges lingered, with newsletters mentioning that 'members interested in joining the Colfax Lodge, which meets and discusses Society affairs at the Russell Street headquarters, can enquire about membership by ringing . . .'[7]

Pickersgill and the board staunchly defended the friendly society model while acknowledging changing times. In the November 1986 *IOOF Update* newsletter, Pickersgill said:

~

Indeed, IOOF holds a unique position in the modern commercial world. It is Australia's largest friendly society, with tens of thousands of members/clients looking upon it as a solid, successful financial institution providing a variety of needed services for them and their families . . . However, to be successful in the 1980s, efficiency is critical, not only to give satisfaction to you as clients, but to survive in the midst of the very competitive commercial world.[8]

~

The *Friendly Societies (Victoria) Act*, proclaimed on 1 September 1987, incorporated that state's first comprehensive review of friendly society legislation. 'The greatest benefit of the new Act is that it allows IOOF to expand its product range and to market this professionally,' Pickersgill said in the *IOOF Investment Update* for November–December 1987.

A member of the Act Review Committee from 1984 to 1987, Pickersgill knew the legislation inside out. The new framework enabled more opportunities but presented challenges, particularly from banks and life insurance offices setting up faux friendly societies. 'A friendly society is more than just an insurance company—it's a whole social welfare framework. Unfortunately, few of the newer friendly societies have the extensive range of bona fide services offered by groups such as ours,' Pickersgill warned in the newsletter.

Investment funds were growing rapidly, and expansion was apace in other fields. IOOF centralised its head office administration, invested around $1 million in computer systems in 1987, and purchased Advance Bank's equity interest in the Security Permanent Building Society, with assets of $134 million after consolidating the World Permanent, Ballarat Permanent and Ararat Permanent Building Societies.

The organisation had grown across all financial and operational measures since Pickersgill's arrival and was in good shape. Australia was emerging from the early 1980s recession, with federal treasurer Paul Keating earning plaudits for his economic stewardship. By introducing the dividend imputation system in 1987, friendly societies gained the right to invest in Australian shares, enabling IOOF to offer diversified investment bonds to existing and new members.

The investments team significantly impacted the organisation's future strategic direction and financial performance. Partnerships with other financial services providers also strengthened the performance of IOOF's products. The BT Investment Bond, operated in conjunction with Bankers Trust, returned 14.6 per cent (after tax) in 1986/87, compared with 13.1 per cent by the Macquarie bond, 12.6 per cent by the standard IOOF bond and 12.5 per cent by the OST Accumulator bond.

IOOF launched a TV advertising campaign in June 1987, created by Leonardi & Curtis and popularly known as the 'roller-coaster ad'. It encouraged consumers to value secure investments rather than chase speculative returns. The timing of this paean to prudence could not have been better for IOOF. The ebullient 1980s crashed on 19 October 1987. The Dow Jones Industrial Average dropped by 22.6 per cent in a single trading session, still the biggest one-day stock market percentage decline in history. By the end of the month, the ASX had lost an astounding 41.8 per cent of its value.

As a safe haven for investors, friendly societies remained sheltered from the worst of the initial fallout. They were popular with those looking to park their money safely while stocks were in freefall. The speed of new funds flowing into IOOF during the last quarter of 1987 was such that administration staff worked around the clock to process applications and bank monies. Investors parked around $380 million with IOOF between July and December 1987, the largest percentage of that coming in the last quarter of the calendar year. The Herculean effort led to the cancellation of the annual staff Christmas Ball that year.

Pickersgill and the IOOF board were navigating an increasingly complex landscape. The Australian economy felt the fallout from the

1987 crash for at least the next five years. Global market corrections and domestic political realities ushered in a period of pessimism. For a brief moment, though, with the financial world in chaos, friendly societies had their chance to shine. Pickersgill and the IOOF board moved quickly to capitalise.

The Pyramid Building Society collapse in July 1990 led to demonstrations against the Victorian Government. IOOF briefly considered acquiring Pyramid before its collapse. Andrew de la Rue/*The Age*

CHAPTER 7

TEMPERANCE
AND TAKEOVERS

✳

I n the last quarter of 1987, new funds continued to pour into Supersaver because of the stock market collapse. Investors also sought to factor in tighter pension-income test rules, which came into force on 1 January 1988. On the back of this momentum, Pickersgill and his team struck while the iron was hot and rolled out fresh offerings to the marketplace.

Attempting to attract new investors, IOOF launched three superannuation products in March 1988. The superannuation industry was still in its infancy, and the leading players were the established life offices, especially AMP and National Mutual. The federal Labor government planted the seeds for the super industry with the revised Prices and Incomes Accord agreement in September 1985. The 1989 retirement income policy statement established the 'twin pillars' of the old-age pension and private superannuation, explicitly rejecting a National Superannuation Scheme. Government policy demarcated industry superfunds and private-sector funds managers.

Eased restrictions on investments helped friendly societies create a broader range of products. New rules in Victoria, where the most prominent societies were based, now allowed an investor to park up to $150,000 in the investment bond of a single society; the previous limit was $50,000. The same legislation contained a provision allowing the state treasurer to approve investment by a friendly society in a range of securities, including shares. However, the October 1987 crash had dampened the benefits of that legislation, at least for a while.

Finance journalist Peter Freeman wrote in February 1988 of the societies: 'Friendly societies, until recently quaint anachronisms of the past, are continuing their rapid growth.'[1] The fastest-growing societies in Victoria were IOOF and the Order of the Sons of Temperance, better known as OST. Neither was a 'quaint anachronism' anymore. Freeman wrote two months later: 'Only the giants of the friendly society industry, such as IOOF, can be expected to be a force in the financial system in the coming decade.'[2]

The longer-term influence of the 1981 Campbell Inquiry was the streamlining of the regulatory regimes governing the activities of non-bank financial institutions like friendly societies. In the same spirit, the 1987 Victorian *Friendly Societies Act* encouraged more competition in the sector. Victorian-based societies could diversify investments, including shares and property, whereas their interstate counterparts were still restricted to fixed-interest investments. The powerful Victorian-based societies, including IOOF, brokered deals with interstate financial institutions to deliver products in accordance with state-based regulations, expanding their reach nationwide.

During 1988, five Victorian societies released managed bonds, including IOOF, OST, the Over 50s Friendly Society, Manchester Unity and the ANA. These products carried a nominally higher level of risk than traditional capital-guaranteed products but also potentially higher returns due to their balanced spread of investments and dividend imputation from equities. IOOF launched the IOOF Managed Bond in May, and by September the fund had grown to $8 million. In the December 1988 *IOOF Investment Update* newsletter, IOOF's General Manager for Investment, Tony Hodges, outlined the objective of the managed bond: 'to achieve consistently above average returns over the life of the policy while seeking to maximise the security of investors' funds through generally conservative investment strategies.'[3]

The launch of this first friendly society managed bond coincided with the start of a new tax regime. The federal mini-budget announced in May 1988 increased the tax rate for societies rise from 20 per cent to 30 per cent. The 20 per cent tax rate on earnings had given friendly societies a significant edge over insurance offices, which incurred a 35 per cent tax rate. In the wake of the mini-budget, friendly societies had to pay 30 per cent tax on all profits, and insurance companies 39 per cent. The tax rate hike pressured societies to lift their performance to continue attracting funds. In June, IOOF began offering share market–linked investments, signalling greater competition between the societies and life offices.

Opening up equity investment offset some damage from a higher tax rate. Funds management switched IOOF from a custodial to a growth mindset. Suddenly, it was about more than safe investments; products could offer higher growth. It certainly broadened the ambition of the IOOF investments team. However, this change left the struggling smaller societies in peril. They needed more funds and the expertise to offer such products and compete, but few had the appetite or the organisational infrastructure to do so.

In December 1988, one of these smaller societies, the Melbourne-based Protestant Alliance (PA), was the subject of a report that questioned its sustainability and highlighted the trouble smaller friendlies were experiencing. These smaller societies were close to extinction, with a shallow pool of reserves and low member numbers. Media reports speculated OST and IOOF were called upon to rescue PA. However, PA soon merged with another Melbourne-based society, the Over 50s Friendly Society. The Queensland-based arm of PA combined operations with the IOOF-backed Community Benefits Association in March 1989, ultimately forming the Sunshine State's largest friendly society, the Community Benefits Association of Queensland Friendly Society

In May 1989, IOOF closed its incredibly successful $1.2-billion Supersaver fund. The fund was heading towards a historically low return of 6 per cent for the 1988/89 financial year, compared to the average return of 12.37 per cent produced over the previous five years. The low forecast returns were in line with most friendly society bonds, with the returns for other bonds ranging from 5 per cent to 9 per cent. The two main reasons for this change were the federal government's increased tax rate on earnings and the Victorian government's new valuation methods, which meant IOOF could not distribute the fund's full earnings. A new fund, Supersaver 2, promptly supplemented Supersaver 1.

The investment team developed new products to capitalise on the solid base provided by Supersaver. The IOOF Defined Benefit Fund #1 launched in June 1989 and raised $80 million fully subscribed. The fund's principal asset was a significant holding, reported as 13.18 per cent, in the Victorian Equity Trust (VET). The fund's defined benefit guaranteed investors a 17 per cent annual compound return upon maturity in 1992. The VET was a Victorian government vehicle that raised $500 million to invest in the State Electricity Commission, the Gas and Fuel Corporation, the Melbourne and Metropolitan Board of Works and the Portland Smelter Unit Trust. Under the scheme, investors were offered $1 shares in the trust, designed to raise equity capital to help the government service debts and invest in capital works. In June, Pickersgill failed to gain election to the VET's management advisory board.

IOOF moved into property trusts in 1989, when it launched a split property trust to give smaller investors exposure to CBD real estate. It focused on city-centre locations and offered investors a hedge against inflation. It was the first to be provided by a friendly society. The first two investments were Sydney properties Grosvenor Place and One O'Connell Street.

Superannuation rule changes in the 1989 federal budget provided a further fillip. Treasurer Paul Keating delivered an unexpected boost by enabling generous concessions to those who took their superannuation payout as a pension rather than a lump sum. The move encouraged the societies to persist with their super schemes, another part of IOOF's emerging funds management strategy.

IOOF boosted group assets by 18 per cent to $2.4 billion in 1989, placing it 128th among Australia's largest 500 companies in assets. It attracted $409 million in new funds during the year, with 63 per cent 'coming from relatively young investors', according to that year's annual report. At the same time, retirees boosted funds invested in the IOOF-approved deposit fund by 27 per cent to $191 million. IOOF Supersaver 2 returned 13.43 per cent after tax, while the IOOF Superannuation Fund earned an after-tax return of 16.09 per cent for the financial year. IOOF's equity funds under management went from zero to $95 million, an impressive result considering investor skittishness following the 1987 crash.

IOOF's approach appeared conservative next to the more adventurous ANA and OST. In the case of OST, it drew on 75 per cent of its $10 million reserves to boost the returns on its Accumulator and Indexed Bond Mark 1, an approach that soon earned the ire of the Victorian Registrar of Friendly Societies.

The 1989 IOOF annual report also noted the successful consolidation of Melbourne city-centre operations in the refurbished Bourke Street office. It also mentioned IOOF Travel having its most successful year to date, while IOOF Retirement Care received the 1989 Residential Care Award from the Victorian Council on the Ageing. Aged-care services were vital to the organisation's offerings: 'The Group intends to become the industry leader, not only in the size of its retirement care operation but also in the quality of service provided.'

IOOF was now a diversified and successful company—'the largest friendly society in Australia', as Blainey notes.[4] It approached the new decade optimistic enough to take out a twelve-year lease for office space at 190 City Road, South Melbourne, at an initial annual rent of $540,000. In Pickersgill's time, employee numbers had risen remarkably, from 60 to nearly 400. Outside the Russell Street headquarters and the Bourke Street offices, there was a desperate need for more space to accommodate the growing IOOF family. That family was about to experience another addition.

By the start of the 1990s, OST was going head to head with IOOF, marketing bonds to conservative smaller investors, who were the bread and butter of friendly societies. Like IOOF, OST had emerged in colonial Australia in the late 1840s. Founded in New York in 1842, it soon spread throughout the north-east United States before expanding to the United Kingdom, Australia and New Zealand. Accounts vary on exactly when OST arrived here. Dr William Hobbs, a Nova Scotia–born Baptist minister, is thought to have introduced the order to Australia and established its first lodge in Sydney sometime in the 1840s. The first Melbourne lodge was established in 1861. As the order's name implies, its raison d'être was temperance, explicitly abstinence from alcohol. Its motto was 'Love, Purity, and Fidelity'. Initiates pledged not to 'make, buy, sell, nor use as a beverage, any spirituous or malt liquors, wine or cider'.[5]

OST advertised itself as 'Australia's friendliest Friendly Society'. Under the leadership of Bob Setterfield, it was one of the top-performing friendly society bond providers and expanded into higher-risk areas like commercial property, including tourism, leisure and hospitality. Alongside his position at OST, Setterfield was also elected president of the Victorian Friendly Societies Association in late 1987. The once-middling OST was now a force in Victoria, investing in a dazzling array of fast-growth ventures. Enter Dreamworld.

News emerged in March 1990 that an advertising agency was taking legal action over the payment of $500,000 owed by the Gold Coast theme park Dreamworld. An article in the *Australian Financial Review* drew attention to the financial pressures caused by the pilots' dispute and high-interest rates on tourism attractions like Dreamworld, but also on OST, which had financed young Queensland entrepreneur Bruce Jenkins' acquisition of the theme park. 'Standing behind Dreamworld is a remarkable finance package involving one of Australia's most aggressively marketed friendly societies—OST, traditionally a shelter for conservative, and often elderly, investors,' reported the *Australian Financial Review*.[6]

The report also highlighted the gulf in salaries between OST and IOOF. One OST director 'earned between $810,000 and $819,999, and the next highest between $470,000 and $479,999', stated the report.

~

However, a survey of the industry shows that top salaries at the OST are much higher than those elsewhere. The IOOF, the biggest friendly society in Australia, is twice the size of the OST. The highest salary earner, presumably chief Martyn Pickersgill, is paid $160,000–170,000. Its second-highest salary earner is on $140,000–150,000.[7]

~

Many felt something was amiss. The Dreamworld deal attracted concern in some quarters, too. Alarms rang when the Estate Mortgage Group, with more than $1 billion in assets, collapsed in April when the Victorian Corporate Affairs Commission froze redemptions from its trusts. Regulators were on heightened alert to problems within the non-bank finance sector against the backdrop of the Victorian government's ongoing woes with the Victorian Economic Development Corporation (VEDC), the State Bank and its merchant bank arm, Tricontinental.

In May, Pickersgill addressed the Victorian Friendly Societies Association's annual conference. As IOOF managing director and the Australian Association of Friendly Societies president, he tried to reassure investors their funds were safe. 'An Estate Mortgage situation could not arise within the [Victorian] member group because . . . all societies are highly liquid and therefore able to meet future demands,' he said.[8] The article reporting Pickersgill's speech noted that he 'may also have been casting an eye on friendly bond-holders anxious about the ramification of the OST affair. OST Friendly Society, one of Victoria's largest, has been the subject of adverse publicity recently over its $152 million loan and loan guarantee to the Gold Coast fun park, Dreamworld'.[9]

The pressure was building on the entire industry and the Victorian government. Things moved quickly over the next two weeks. On 1 July 1990, the administrator liquidated the Farrow Group, which included the Pyramid Building Society and several smaller businesses. Anger with the Farrow Group and the Victorian government was widespread. Public protests were virulent, with reports of tens of thousands expressing their discontent at public demonstrations, some even going as far as bringing along effigies of the Victorian premier, John Cain.

An *Australian Financial Review* report on 6 July 1990 raised the prospect of a merger. Pickersgill responded to the rumour: 'A merger is not a decision that the chief executives of the groups are authorised to make. It is a decision that will be made by both boards and by the Registrar of Friendly Societies.'[10] OST stayed quiet: 'OST's general manager (corporate planning), Mr Ken Stonehouse, denied any merger talks were taking place and said merger rumours were being fed by a lunchtime meeting between OST, IOOF and the Victorian Treasurer, Mr Roper.'[11]

The next day, *The Age* announced that merger talks were underway. Another report said spooked OST investors had withdrawn an estimated $10 million in funds the previous week. The *Australian Financial Review* reported that the 'proposed merger has the hallmarks of a takeover-cum-rescue. The OST name will no longer exist, and the new entity will trade as the IOOF Financial Group following a major rationalisation operation.'[12]

Despite protests by OST management, the $3.7-billion merger proceeded. On 12 July 1990, the Order of the Sons of Temperance National Division Friendly Society merged with the IOOF of Victoria Friendly Society, increasing group funds under management by $981 million for the IOOF group.

Joan Kirner took over as Victoria's Premier from John Cain in August 1990 but she could not turn the Labor Party's fortunes around. IOOF had a rocky relationship with the state Labor government. *The Sydney Morning Herald*

The next few weeks were frantic. 'It was all hands on deck, but we strongly believed in our culture,' recalled Sue Herrald, a long-time IOOF and Insignia Financial employee. She said IOOF and OST had very different cultures. 'We left the Bouverie Street office and had taken over the OST building in Alma Road. At IOOF, we never wasted money. When we moved to Alma Road, we could not believe the opulence, the mahogany walls and such, and we thought, "This is why we are still in business!"'

Sadly, after a celebratory board dinner in Carlton on the night the takeover was sealed, IOOF director Jim Meneilly collapsed on the footpath and died. Meneilly was a longstanding member of IOOF, a Grand Treasurer, twice Grand Master and a stalwart of the Loyal Bentleigh Lodge.

Meneilly was a link to a past of ceremonies and traditions that had faded from view as IOOF embraced its future as a financial services business. The Tip Top Poultry business manager and Eastern Suburbs Churches Football Association president had a strong business sense. Blainey praised Meneilly's role in keeping IOOF alive during the late 1970s:

~

He was valuable because he had sufficient business experience to identify the problems of the IOOF and the quality of leadership which, twice earning him the post of Grand Master, was urgently needed in the crisis. He counted it no trouble to arrive at the head office of IOOF evening after evening, after his own day's work was over, to discuss the difficulties, and even sign the cheques.[13]

~

IOOF's history is full of leaders like Meneilly, who passed on the ethos of service to a new generation of leaders, including Martyn Pickersgill, Tony Hodges, Philip Fraher and Kevin Homewood. Their values were a source of strength for the organisation, even if they sometimes limited its commercial opportunities.

Meneilly's death and the merger symbolised the transition from one era to the next. IOOF now had to consider the wellbeing of its members and of those it had inherited from OST. As in 1983, with the takeover of Hibernians, IOOF was reluctantly rescuing an ailing rival. Hibernians had been a relatively painless takeover; OST was trickier.

Journalist Peter Freeman wrote in *The Age* of an unenviable task ahead: 'For IOOF investors, the question is whether the society, by coming to the aid of the industry as a whole, has taken on problems of such magnitude that its own long-term performance will be adversely affected.'[14]

But Freeman was confident IOOF's track record would see it through: 'On the basis of my understanding of IOOF's financial position, as well as the quality of its management, there is no logical reason why the takeover of OST should adversely affect IOOF investors. If it does, it will be because of an unjustified panic by investors.'[15]

Along with others in Victorian business and government circles, IOOF recognised the severe repercussions were OST to collapse and go the way of Estate Mortgage, Tricontinental and Pyramid. In *The Canberra Times*, journalist Helen Corcoran wrote: 'The collapse of Victoria's financial institutions rocked the state like no other event in 1990. In a spectacular and truly frightening few months this year, Victorians saw the very foundations of their financial system undermined.'[16]

The string of collapses put enormous pressure on prudent organisations like IOOF. Public suspicions of financial misconduct in general were high, and trust was low. If OST collapsed in the same month as Pyramid—on top of all the other turmoil heaped upon the state—the state's economy would have faced a meltdown. IOOF chair David Jury spoke plainly in the 1991 annual report: 'A critical loss of confidence in Australia's economy during the first quarter provided the impetus for what proved an unforgiving 1990/91 fiscal year. The period was highlighted by record levels of business failure and unemployment not seen in Australia for many years.'

Victorian premier John Cain resigned on 7 August 1990, with Joan Kirner becoming Australia's third female head of government and second female premier. Her government sold the State Bank of Victoria to the Commonwealth Bank for $1.6 billion. It opened an inquiry into the $2.7-billion losses of the bank's failed merchant arm, Tricontinental. But Kirner could not redeem Labor and suffered a landslide defeat by the Jeff Kennett–led Liberal–National coalition at the 1992 election.

Former Reserve Bank governor Ian Macfarlane said in his 2006 Boyer Lectures: 'I believe that the financial excesses of the 1980s reached such a scale that the 1990 recession was inevitable.' He noted 'that any boom built on rising asset prices financed by increased borrowing has to end'.[17] OST and Dreamworld provided an example of Macfarlane's point.

With the economy in the doldrums and tasked with integrating OST and dealing with its loan book, Pickersgill and IOOF faced a difficult road ahead.

IOOF expanded into retirement homes in the 1980s as part of a strategy to serve the needs of its ageing members. The organisation had four such homes before selling out of the sector. City of Melbourne Libraries

IOOF's Russell Street headquarters in Melbourne had been a mainstay since the foundation stone for the main building was laid in 1872. It was sold by IOOF in 1993 and is now residential apartments. Peter Wille/State Library of Victoria

CHAPTER 8

IOOF AT THE
CROSSROADS

✳

The OST takeover gave IOOF some colourful assets. 'We were in control of Lasseters casino in Alice Springs, Dreamworld on the Gold Coast,' Sue Herrald recalled. 'The standing joke at the time was that one of the only paying mortgages in the mortgage fund was a brothel in Kalgoorlie!'

The surreal nature of the takeover presented moments of black comedy. 'It is with regret that the executive committee of the OST Friendly Society has decided to postpone the Bush Dance, which was to have been held at the Lawn Tennis Association, Brisbane, on Friday,' IOOF instructed OST members. 'We regret the necessity for the postponement, but we assure (dear members) every effort will be made to continue Fraternal Activities in the near future.'[1]

Initially, many worried that IOOF had bitten off more than it could chew. Running the investments division, Tony Hodges was shocked at the scale of mismanagement he had inherited:

~

We took on 90 mortgage loans over every type of tourist operation around, particularly northern Australia. This was in the aftermath of the pilots' strike and a downturn in domestic tourism. Northern Australia was decimated. And then there was, of course, corrupt brokers, lax lenders, corrupt borrowers, etc. That was when the Corporate Crimes Squad actually started in Victoria. OST was its first case.

~

But Hodges said things could have been worse. IOOF had quietly looked at acquiring the Pyramid Building Society only weeks before it collapsed. 'We spent a whole week doing due diligence on taking over Pyramid,' Hodges recalled. 'Thankfully, we didn't pursue that.'

At takeover, there was a spread of around 90 mortgages across three frozen OST funds, accounting for about $390 million in principal lending by OST, mainly secured on tourism and commercial properties. Hodges estimated that up to 98 per cent of these mortgages were either non-performing or in default. The Dreamco loans totalled $158 million, and the Lasseters casino loan was $33 million. The size of these loans required a funds freeze until management could review and formulate a plan to liquidate, recoup costs or rehabilitate the funds.

The late 1980s recession hit many people hard and led to business collapses and high rates of unemployment. Rick Stevens/*The Sydney Morning Herald*

IOOF had emerged as the white knight of the friendly society sector but at a cost. Pickersgill and his team faced salvaging what they could from the OST assets, endeavouring to deliver a fair and reasonable outcome for investors, and integrating the productive remnants into IOOF. All this as the Victorian economy was struggling through its worst crisis since the 1890s.

At the time, unfounded rumours circulated about the imminent collapse of the Bank of Melbourne, spooking OST investors already worried about their funds disappearing. IOOF reassured OST members that their money was safe in a series of town hall meetings. Over the next six months, IOOF worked hard to reassure OST investors.

In 1986, IOOF had $705 million in funds under management. By 1991, that figure was $3.6 billion. The popularity of products like Supersaver boosted membership over those five years from 75,000 to 320,000. Staff numbers increased to 750, with offices in all states except Tasmania. Beyond its core businesses, the group expanded into travel, retirement and financial planning. IOOF was now the largest friendly society in Australia.[2]

The Victorian crisis had raised serious questions about the non-bank financial sector that had flourished in the deregulatory environment fostered by the Hawke/Keating government. An editorial in *The Age* from 18 July 1990 questioned the long-term sustainability of building and friendly societies:

~

The prudently managed building societies and friendly societies will come through the present difficulties. Their long-term position, however, is more complicated. Historically, they owe their place in the market in large measure to the high degree of regulation of the Australian banking system, which has changed only recently. It is no surprise, then, that some building societies and co-operatives should have problems in this first difficult investment period since the deregulation of the banks. Those with problems are the ones which have imprudently begun acting out of character—and have been allowed to do so by inadequate government supervision.[3]

~

IOOF steadily diversified its products, particularly in trustee services, financial advice, and retirement planning and services. Within IOOF, some questioned the organisation's long-term structure. Murmurs about demutualisation could be heard. The business was growing, but some thought its friendly society status was hindering its potential.

Perhaps overlooked amid the headline-making merger with OST was the Adelaide-based IEL Trustee Group acquisition in June 1990, which increased IOOF's total asset base by around $400 million. It gave IOOF a stronger foothold in trustee services and expanded the group's operations in South Australia. The acquisition signalled IOOF's intent to become a significant player in the trustee services sector.

Alongside this, IOOF gave its financial planning arm more autonomy, signalled by its renaming from IOOF Financial Planning to Winchcombe Carson Financial Planning, a name derived from one of the three trustee companies owned by IOOF.

IOOF started 1991 well, reporting $125 million in new premiums for the first half of the financial year. The Defined Benefit Fund 2 launch in October 1990 played a big part in the positive result, reaching $80 million in subscribers. The performance of the IOOF Building Society was another positive, with 20 per cent of new funds attributable to new loans written.

However, the VET had created a rift between IOOF and the state government. A report surfaced at the end of January 1991, publicising unit holders' concerns about the state government's failure to clarify the trust's redemption date despite repeated queries. It highlighted the tense relationship between the state Labor government and IOOF, with IOOF publicly criticising the government for 'not coming clean' on the matter.[4]

A good relationship with the state government of the day had always been imperative for IOOF. After the OST rescue, IOOF felt state treasurer Tom Roper could have been more forthcoming on details about the VET. After months of no response, IOOF and the other big unit holders—including the AMP Society, National Mutual and the State Superannuation Board of Victoria—had written to the government in early December 1991 in relation to the progress of the $750-million VET payouts. The ASX had also sent the state government a 'please explain' letter, asking when it planned to pay out investors in the state-backed trust. Eventually, the unit holders took the matter to the media to force the government's hand.

OST continued to take up time and energy for Pickersgill and his team. Victoria Police's Corporate Crime Division started investigations targeting OST executives, including Bob Setterfield, and Dreamworld's former owner Bruce Jenkins. IOOF extended the funds freeze, as poor returns from property sales had failed to lift liquidity adequately. The freeze would be reviewed again in mid-1992.

In April 1991, IOOF issued several writs to Jenkins, with some related to his personally guaranteed debt, which exceeded $102 million. IOOF was in litigation with the former OST directors and Jenkins. In October 1991, the police opened another investigation into the loss of at least $200 million, possibly as much as $600 million, from OST.

After the 1990 state crisis, IOOF consistently reassured the public it was a safe investment option. One ad proclaimed: 'We're not a bank . . . we're not a building society . . . we're not an insurance company . . . we're IOOF, which is better than all of those put together.'

The friendly society sector had been depleted by the Victorian crisis but the stronger societies, such as IOOF, managed to prove many of the naysayers wrong. Writing in *The Age* in 1991, finance journalist Peter Freeman once more commended IOOF:

~

Yet today, almost a year later, the friendly movement is able to point to the fact that it was able to weather the setback. Although most of the credit belongs to IOOF and its chief executive, Mr Martyn Pickersgill, the movement's ability to cope with the demise of OST—then the second biggest friendly society in Australia—is an important indicator of the solid foundations of the main friendly society bonds.[5]

~

But how long would IOOF remain a friendly society? In July 1991, IOOF discussed becoming a life office with the Insurance and Superannuation Commission. Capital formation restrictions hampered IOOF's ability to fulfil its ambitions as a friendly society. 'We would prefer to remain as a friendly society with a mutual base—that's the basis of our culture,' Pickersgill told *The Age*. 'But that's providing the legislative control allows us to offer the services the clients want. If that changes, the alternative is to change to a life company.'[6]

In November 1991, IOOF posted an operating deficit of $4.4 million after writing off $34.3 million for OST Friendly Society mortgage portfolio losses. The deficit compared with a surplus of $181.76 million the previous year. The surplus and deficit accounts were compiled under life insurance accounting standards; on a conventional basis, IOOF made a $5.6-million trading profit that year, compared with a $4.2-million profit the previous year.

A significant highlight of 1991 was Winchcombe Carson's appointment as a preferred financial planner by the ACTU, a considerable coup. Another important event during 1991 was IOOF becoming the freehold owner of its historical head office at 380 Russell Street. The property had been subject to a Crown grant. IOOF revalued the property, adding $3 million to the group's asset revaluation reserve, despite a depressed property market.

The year ended on a down note, with the credit agency Moody's Investor Service warning about the risks involved in investing in friendly societies. In its report entitled *Australian Friendly Societies:*

Growth amid Uncertainties, Moody's said the sector's regulatory framework lacked clarity and could be detrimental to investors. Pickersgill called Moody's actions 'irresponsible scare tactics that threaten to unduly worry investors and to destabilise the industry'.[7]

The halcyon days for friendly societies seemed over, but IOOF continued to attract investors looking for safe, tax-effective returns. Pickersgill publicly defended the sector, but internally the sentiment for change grew.

The financial services industry was undergoing evaluation and reappraisal, with a raft of inquiries initiated by state governments spooked by the events in Victoria. The Reserve Bank's 1991 annual report highlighted the possibility of increased oversight and regulation of friendlies: 'There is also considerable momentum for prudential reform in the funds management industry, including life offices and superannuation funds, friendly societies, and unit trusts.'[8]

IOOF observed such overtures. Group General Manager Kevin Homewood noted in the 1991 annual report:

~

Although IOOF is supportive of the need to review and protect the interests of investors, we are concerned about the lack of understanding of our structure and businesses. We are also concerned about the direction of government review which seems to be heading towards an undue and unwelcome restriction of our operations.

~

In 1992, IOOF continued to battle with the state government over the VET. The Barclay's Bank subsidiary BZW Australia and IOOF secured two of the five effective board seats on the trust. The move put additional pressure on the struggling state government. Victorian public-sector net debt had ballooned to $31.7 billion by mid-1992. Unemployment was around 11 per cent, and youth unemployment was 46 per cent.

After the VET initially brought the state government some success, it unravelled. The government wound up the scheme and paid out investors, adding a further $710 million to the state's debt. It was one less thing on the plate for IOOF, as it tended to OST matters, both financial and legal, plus the array of businesses it was now involved in, including retirement villages.

By June 1992, construction was underway on the IOOF Keperra Sanctuary Retirement Village in Brisbane, the fourth such village built by IOOF. The others were Cumberland View, the Riverwood Village at Albury and the IOOF Glendale Aged Care Hostel at Werribee in Melbourne's south-west. Plans were afoot for more. The IOOF Retirement Care business was promising, with assets increasing to $100 million and sales of 102 retirement units valued at $11.2 million over the past year.

Was the future of IOOF in running retirement villages, which brought it a captive audience for ancillary services like travel, health and financial planning? Or would IOOF become a life insurance company, with retirement homes thrown into the mix? In the 1992 annual report, Pickersgill again addressed the matter:

~

In the light of these changes to capital requirements, regulation and reserving levels, the IOOF Australia Group is undertaking a review to determine the options for the next decade. As part of this review IOOF is considering the Insurance and Superannuation Commissions as a potential alternate regulator. The aim of this review is to determine the best way of meeting new capital, reserving and regulatory requirements while maximising return and security for members. This review will only recommend changes that are clearly in the best interest of members. No decisions will be made that would jeopardise member investments.

~

IOOF was at a crossroads. It was becoming a big business, but of what kind? The threat of irrelevance in the 1970s had driven a 'diversify or die' strategy during the 1980s. The prosperity of the 1980s meant IOOF could participate in several sectors and bear minor losses. The success of Supersaver funded these enterprising explorations. However, the early 1990s put a brake on this untrammelled growth.

After the painful previous few years, things started to look up again. IOOF's capital-guaranteed deferred annuity fund returned a healthy 11.2 per cent, the capital-guaranteed fixed-interest fund also returned 11.2 per cent, and the group's managed investment trust yielded 15.93 per cent. The superannuation bond earned 12 per cent, the managed flexi bond 8.62 per cent, and the mortgage flexi bond

9.49 per cent. The capital stable super bond earned 13.39 per cent. As an organisation, IOOF managed 5 per cent asset growth in a year when other institutions were experiencing investor withdrawals. The results underlined the organisation's steady management and improvement in the economy, with inflation kept in check. The worst of the early-1990s recession was starting to fade.

The October 1992 state election delivered the Jeff Kennett–led Liberal–National coalition a landslide victory. The result released a pressure valve for IOOF, ending its relationship with the Labor government, which had been, at times, challenging. By the end of 1992, IOOF had $4.5 billion in funds under management and around 348,000 members, making it far larger than its nearest competitor, the Over 50s Friendly Society, with about 140,000 members.

IOOF established IOOF Investment Management Ltd (IIML) to handle its funds and wholesale funds from other sources. IOOF appointed three external directors to oversee IIML—Duncan Andrews, the founder of Australian Ratings; Lindsay Bytheway, finance director of Mayne Nickless; and Dr Roger Sexton, managing director of Beston Pacific Corporation. With 802 employees nationally, IOOF looked less like a friendly society of old and more like a financial institution with heft.

In December 1992, the Victorian Financial Institutions Commission (VicFIC) approved three-year freeze extensions on the three OST member benefit funds. The partial freeze gave members limited access to those funds, with term maturities and death payments made as required. The slow economy did not help IOOF offload assets like Dreamworld or the other residual OST assets. The continuing criminal investigations also soured interest among potential buyers for Dreamworld, which had continued to trade well despite difficult times for tourism. Of the 114 mortgages held by the OST funds when IOOF took over in 1990, seventeen remained, all cashflow-positive and providing returns.

IOOF placed one of the other OST assets, Lasseters Hotel Casino in Alice Springs, into receivership in mid-1993. While operating at a profit, it still couldn't cover its debt repayments. In the meantime, it had earned a footnote in Australian film history by serving as a location in the hugely successful *The Adventures of Priscilla, Queen of the Desert*, released in 1994.

Reflecting on the merger with OST, Tony Hodges said: 'That really shaped IOOF's path for a good ten-year period, which wasn't

Lasseters Casino in Alice Springs was acquired by IOOF when it took over the OST Friendly Society. IOOF managed assets such as Lasseters and Dreamworld until suitable buyers were found. Bahnfrend/Wikimedia Commons

necessarily great. You put the two together and got a $4 billion organisation, which got headlines in the paper. The reality was half of it was only ever going to be a liquidation.'

Midway through 1993, a slice of IOOF history ended when the 380 Russell Street head office was sold to a Singaporean buyer for $2.8 million. The building became residential accommodation. In September 1993, old rivals Manchester Unity and the ANA announced their merger. As the third-biggest and fourth-biggest friendly societies, the merged entity was worth nearly $1 billion and became Australian Unity, focusing on health insurance.

The 1993 federal budget announced a gradual hike in the tax rate on friendlies: from 30 per cent to 33 per cent in the 1994/95 financial year, 36 per cent in 1995/96, and 39 per cent by 1996/97. The tax advantages once enjoyed by friendly societies were gone. The business was morphing into a different entity.

IOOF's 1992/93 financial year results were a mixed bag. Investment earnings fell away due to falling interest rates, and despite a small sales rise to compensate, the operating surplus was only a quarter the size of the previous year's. The surplus—effectively, a profit—was $58.9 million, compared with $236.9 million. Falling interest rates had reduced earnings. The management fund surplus dropped from $6.3 million to $4.1 million, attributed to restructuring costs, which included significant redundancy payouts.

OST put a considerable drag on forward momentum. Promising diversification strategies were beginning to look challenging. Investment and funds management held its own, but health and travel looked awkward fits for an organisation identifying itself as a significant funds manager.

Commenting on the turmoil of 1990 in the *IOOF Update* newsletter, Pickersgill said:

~

From that difficult period, IOOF emerged with its other assets intact and profitable. The loyalty of IOOF members and OST members provided the support we needed to restructure portfolios. The response from members gave us a feeling that we had achieved something worthwhile.[9]

~

Speaking about IOOF's future, Pickersgill reiterated the friendly society ethos of independence and self-help:

~

The focus for IOOF remains that of creating real wealth for members so that they are not dependent on the public purse when they are no longer working. Such wealth creates independence and provides more choices in what people want to do with their lives particularly in retirement. This is what we are really all about.[10]

~

Speaking about the organisation's challenges, he again asserted the primacy of the friendly society structure, but with a caveat:

~

The prime entity in the group is the friendly society, and the friendlies are going through a major review by the Premiers' Working Party. We need to ensure that if changes are made to current legislation then it will be responsive to the industry's needs. If not, we have to be prepared to take whatever action is necessary to ensure the group continues to offer the right products at the right time to the right people.[11]

~

In September 1994, Pickersgill resigned, citing personal reasons and the need for a new challenge. Under his stewardship, IOOF membership had risen from 25,000 to 350,000, and assets increased from $80 million to more than $4 billion. '[But] it hasn't been without personal cost,' he said in a newspaper report. 'I haven't got anything lined up. I'll be staying until the end of the year, then taking a break to assess where I will go.' He said: 'The organisation needs a change now to take it into its next growth period.'[12]

He was thanked for his services in the 1995 annual report:

~

During 1994/95 our former Managing Director, Martyn Pickersgill, resigned, having been with IOOF for 12 years. During that period, IOOF grew enormously, becoming the major player and leader in the friendly society industry, and Martyn earning a tremendous level of respect from the board for leading IOOF to its position of prominence.

~

Pickersgill's tenure had seen monumental changes and modernisation at IOOF. He inherited a struggling organisation that appeared ready to go the way of many of its fellow friendly societies. His energy, conviction and intelligence had taken IOOF to a new level. He would continue serving the friendly society movement in his next role, as the chief executive of the Friendly Societies Association.

In only a few years, IOOF would undergo more significant changes of a kind many in the industry might never have entertained.

Queensland entrepreneur Bruce Jenkins purchased Dreamworld with funding from the OST Friendly Society. IOOF inherited Dreamworld when OST collapsed and was taken over by IOOF. *Gold Coast Bulletin*

CHAPTER 9

IN A DREAM WORLD

Peter Twigg's duties as the general manager of IOOF's Riverwood Retirement Village in Albury were diverse. Twigg, a former banker with ANZ and Chase AMP, had helped kickstart the investments division in 1985 alongside Tony Hodges.

Working in finance, he had dealt with a snake or two in the past, figuratively speaking. But running a retirement village presented unique challenges. 'Already, I have removed a tiger snake from a resident's unit, a car from a resident's lounge, and was privileged to be MC at the wedding of two residents who met at Riverwood and had their reception here in the Village Community Centre,' he told the December 1995 issue of the IOOF staff newsletter. Twigg's midlife career switch was a tree change for him and his family. 'I don't know if it was the pandemonium that surrounded the OST takeover or not, but it just seemed the time was right for a change.'[1]

IOOF's diversification over the past decade was nearly as varied as Twigg's duties. Taking on the collapsed OST compounded the sense of an organisation searching for focus. By 1994, the structure of the IOOF Australia Group comprised 42 legal entities, including friendly societies, a building society, retirement villages, funds management, a travel agency, various trusts and financial-planning businesses. The group had offices and representation in almost every Australian capital city and many suburban and rural spots, with nineteen retail branches across Victoria.

The organisation had become unwieldy. An IOOF group circular in April 1994 detailed that 'a small committee has therefore been formed . . . with the object of cleaning up the structure of the Group by the rationalisation of funds and entities'. One of Pickersgill's last statements to the media as IOOF CEO hinted at the possible direction of the group. He said IOOF would not become a life office but could list on the stock exchange. For IOOF to move forward, clarity was required. It needed a defined purpose.

With IOOF now one of Australia's top ten funds managers, its board reviewed operations and developed a five-year plan to become a significant retail and wholesale funds management organisation. If IOOF were to challenge the likes of BT, Macquarie and the Commonwealth Bank, it would have to recruit expertise and reinforce operational resources. A former ANZ McCaughan head of research, Russell Barnes, was appointed to head its investment division and strengthen the investment team from nine to sixteen staff. Tony Hodges took on the role of general manager of IIML, working closely with Lindsay Bytheway, Roger Sexton and Duncan Andrews to set an investment strategy for the group.

Technology improvements were also undertaken. Under Ian Gill's leadership as Information Systems General Manager, the organisation's IT infrastructure was upgraded, prioritising data centralisation. A keener focus on IT included working with IBM to overhaul the mainframe computing infrastructure, a sizeable task when the internet, email and off-the-shelf software solutions were in their infancy as workplace tools. IOOF's commitment to IT included sponsoring an event at the Financial Planners' Association's 1995 conference: 'IOOF in conjunction with IBM put the Internet on display. We produced some DL flyers outlining basic terminology and what the Internet is all about,' according to the IOOF staff newsletter. The process of computerisation initiated by Pickersgill in the early 1980s was moving into a new phase.

Meanwhile, the Australian economy continued to be challenging. The dark days of the early 1990s were starting to recede, but economic forecasts remained relatively weak. The Keating government defied the odds to win the 1993 federal election. It instituted programs like Working Nation to tackle stubborn unemployment, alongside a schedule of privatisations to return the budget to surplus. The ALP had been in power since 1983, but support for the Keating government was faltering within the business community.

In Victoria, Jeff Kennett's Coalition government accelerated the privatisation of state assets. It significantly reduced public expenditure, cutting back around 5 per cent of the state public service within a month of winning the October 1992 election. Kennett's approach rubbed some the wrong way. Still, he intended to ensure Victoria was 'on the move' after years of economic paralysis, and this suited business interests.

The downturn in the bond and share markets led to patchy results, including negative returns on some funds in 1994. Shares, which had risen by 40 per cent the previous year, dropped again at the start of 1994 by 10 per cent. Heavily tied to fixed-interest investments, IOOF moved to short-dated securities to prop up returns. Fixed-interest markets globally experienced significant volatility due to an unexpected lift in US bond yields. Returns from fixed-interest investments depended on economic recovery and the inevitable turn in the interest-rate cycle.

The Australian market was affected more extensively by the yo-yo nature of the US market than had been expected.

With Pickersgill's departure from IOOF at the end of 1994, board chair Damien J. Smith assumed the role of executive chair, handling interim CEO duties until Sydney-based Graham Cook joined as CEO in March 1995, whereupon Smith reverted to chair.

Cook's appointment was not seen as a long-term solution. He was on a twelve-month contract as a transitional hand to guide the organisation following Pickersgill's departure. Cook joined IOOF after three years as managing director of the financial services group Le Fort Capital Corp. He was formerly general manager of Chase AMP's consumer banking division.

Cook immediately met with challenges. Within a month, he had to execute the board's plans to slash spending and institute redundancies to fix cashflow problems. The austerity measures included cutting staff numbers by 6 per cent, restricting travel, reducing advertising and stopping the use of outside consultants. These cuts followed similar steps taken in 1993. The main issue was IOOF's operational cashflow. This posed no risk to investors' funds, protected by solvency reserves monitored by VicFIC.

The previous year VicFIC had imposed upon IOOF a $7-million-a-year payment into a special management reserve fund established when shortfalls estimated at $70 million built up in the frozen OST funds. Friendly societies, including IOOF, had struggled to recover after a tough few years, with funds under management across the sector plummeting 10 per cent. The bond market slump and the legal restrictions on external fundraising hampered the friendly society sector's recovery.

Funds retention was also a mounting problem. IOOF had paid out $471.3 million in benefits in the previous financial year, compared with $340.3 million the year before. More money flowed out than came in as people sought to tap into their superannuation and other investments. IOOF was not alone in this predicament. Unprofitable parts of the business were in the firing line as IOOF looked to pivot towards funds management. The tight squeeze on management funds was not as severe as in 1978. Still, it constricted the organisation's capacity to hire new talent and challenge the top-end funds managers.

By mid-1995, a changing of the guard had taken place. Following Pickersgill's departure, two more experienced executives had followed:

Philip Fraher, the group general manager for sales and services, and Kevin Homewood, the group general manager for corporate services. Fraher was also the general manager, funds management. Before that, he had overseen the IOOF Security Permanent Building Society and its fifteen Victorian branches, IOOF Travel, and the White Horse Savings and Loans Co-operative Ltd. Homewood had been with IOOF for seventeen years and had been a vital member of the executive team. He was there during the dark days of the late 1970s and had been an ally to Pickersgill during the organisation's rebuild. An internal group bulletin said Fraher's exit was 'a consequence of both parties recognising their inability to work together and a divergent view of the group's core business strengths and strategic direction'.

Speaking to the media following the departures, Cook said his mandate was to 'process re-engineer' IOOF: 'This will involve building revenue and profitability, establishing an efficient cost base and minimising withdrawals and increasing retentions.'[2] To undertake this re-engineering, however, IOOF still had to tend to the protracted resolution of the OST legacy.

The merger between IOOF and OST in 1990 had led to significant issues. The Dreamworld loans, totalling $158 million, were at

IOOF chair Ray Schoer (left) and chief executive Ron Dewhurst (right) helped establish the business as a listed entity. Schoer previously worked as a corporate regulator. Colin Murty/Newspix

the heart of the issues. Days before the merger, Pickersgill said of Dreamworld: 'We do have a strategy that we have worked out for the Dreamworld exposure.'[3] The original plan was for several friendly societies to spread the risk of the Dreamco loan, but that agreement soon dissolved, forcing IOOF to go it alone and freeze the OST funds. IOOF recovered some funds in 1991 by selling Dreamco's North Queensland Great Adventures assets, including the lease of Green and Fitzroy islands. However, the policy on Dreamworld was one of 'no sale' until a buyer offered a price that met the asset's long-term perceived value.

IOOF and the receivers ensured the adventure park was run profitably to make it attractive to potential buyers. The 1993/94 financial year was one of Dreamworld's most profitable on record. The appointed receivers, Ernst & Young, fielded inquiries, usually leading to nothing. Dreamworld's fundamentals were strong. However, the economy's poor state was not conducive to attracting a suitable buyer to make the sale worthwhile for IOOF or OST investors.

In March 1994, a plan was devised for Dreamworld to be a key asset in a $60-million public float involving a consortium of retail and tourism backers, including Coles Myer. The plan was not able to be implemented after the Australian Securities Commission flagged issues with the prospectus, and former owner Bruce Jenkins issued a vexatious Supreme Court writ seeking repayment of loans of $143 million.

At the time, Pickersgill reiterated IOOF's eagerness to sell the asset. 'Although we have successfully run the park since taking control in July 1990, IOOF's intention has always been to sell the property because running theme parks is not our business,' he told the *Australian Financial Review*.[4] Jenkins' claims backfired in December 1994 when a Queensland court ordered he repay IOOF more than $116 million. Soon after, Jenkins faced bankruptcy proceedings after creditors rejected his offer to pay $20,000 in settlement of debts reported as being up to $431 million to all his creditors.

At the end of January 1995, Victoria Police charged Jenkins with seven charges of conspiracy to defraud concerning loans from OST. Police charged three others with conspiring to dishonestly obtain $31 million from OST by falsely representing valuation reports relating to Lasseters Hotel Casino.

In late 1995, Malaysian poultry entrepreneur Kevin Lau pulled out of a joint $80-million bid with the Queensland-based Koala Corp.

At the start of 1996, despite objections raised by various parties on the grounds of foreign investment, federal treasurer Ralph Willis announced approval for the $85-million sale of Dreamworld to Janola Dale Pty Ltd, a company controlled by Singaporean property developer and tourism operator Kua Phek Long's Euro-Asia Leisure Trust. It had been a long time coming, and a reward for holding out for the right price rather than taking the first offer. Five and a half years after the merger, the Dreamworld roller-coaster ride was over. For IOOF, the sale removed a significant financial and management burden.

The sale enabled IOOF to raise sufficient funds to make the remaining $254 million of frozen assets available in two OST funds. More than 30,000 investors holding about 80,000 policies in OST's accumulator and mortgage bond funds could now access their money. But earnings and the realisation of assets couldn't bridge a shortfall in the funds, so investors' funds were subject to discounts of between 10 per cent and 25 per cent. The vast majority of investors accepted this outcome.

The offer to OST investors made midway through 1996 was among Cook's last pieces of business. He had overseen a period that involved much necessary though difficult housekeeping. Having been hired to guide the organisation after Martyn Pickersgill's long tenure, he had executed his brief and given the IOOF board breathing room to search for a CEO who could execute the longer-term vision.

Between 1994 and 1996, several changes to the board's composition also signalled the group's shift towards funds management and investments. Ray Schoer joined in 1994, replacing Geoff MacFarlane, who had been on the board for nine years. Schoer brought extensive experience in regulatory compliance at the National Companies and Securities Commission and then as the national director of the ASX. Before that, he worked at the Commonwealth Department of Treasury, was assistant secretary to the Commonwealth Department of Business and Consumer Affairs, and was secretary to the Ministerial Council for Companies and Securities.

Roger Sexton joined the board in 1995, having already been involved on the investments side of the business with IIML. Sexton was also the chair of the IOOF Friendly Society of South Australia and the South Australian government's Asset Management Taskforce. He specialised in corporate restructures, mergers and acquisitions, and privatisations.

IOOF ran successful retirement villages, including Riverwood Retirement Home in Albury (pictured), but Lindsay Bytheway did not see them as part of the greater strategic plan. Courtesy of Bolton Clarke

Merran Kelsall joined in 1995 and took on the role of chair of the Group Audit Committee, bringing experience from her time on various boards and as a partner with leading accounting firm BDO Nelson Parkhill.

Lindsay Bytheway joined the board of IIML in 1992 and became a board member of IOOF in 1993. He'd had an extensive executive career with Mayne Nickless.

At the end of 1995, Bytheway and Schoer were appointed as chair and deputy chair, respectively. The board's composition was now more corporate, with more experience in banking and finance than previous boards. Board members now had close experience working with listed companies. A few older faces remained, with David Jury, Ron Bunton and Geoffrey Cayzer providing continuity and stability.

Jury's time with IOOF stretched back to 1960, when he was appointed Lodge Secretary. In subsequent years, he had served in many roles, including as board chair in 1979, 1985, and from 1991 to 1994. He had been a keeper of the flame, a talisman of the organisation's proud tradition of helping people enjoy financial independence for themselves.

During the 1990s, IOOF had experienced much turmoil and lost some key figures who had helped guide the organisation. But a transformed version of IOOF was now taking shape. A new CEO would have to unite a disparate workforce, from retirement village employees to investment analysts, and execute a brave strategy that took IOOF on a new path. Lindsay Bytheway believed he knew just the person for the job.

The push towards financial services industry deregulation was boosted when the Liberal–National coalition, led by John Howard, won the federal election on 2 March 1996. News Ltd

CHAPTER 10

END OF A SAGA

❉

Dreamworld was gone, but the Lasseters casino was still on IOOF's books. The casino's receiver, Deloitte Touche Tohmatsu, had attempted a private sale the year before, but the ongoing OST criminal investigation and assorted legal matters had precluded a sale. Understandably, buyers were nervous with court cases still afoot. A concerted push was made again at the start of 1996, with a goal of obtaining $25 million. A sale would help wind up the OST saga and pump much-needed funds into the IOOF business, which was hurting from the continued exodus of investors from friendly bonds.

Rationalisation in the sector had gathered pace with the merger of the Adelaide-based Lifeplan-Manchester Unity friendly society and the Melbourne-based Investment Action Friendly to create a group with $470 million in assets and about 150,000 members. Other mergers included the PA Friendly Society and the Over 50s, StateGuard and Australian Pacific, and the largest of all, the Victorian Manchester Unity and ANA friendly societies merging to become Australian Unity. The smaller friendlies either became easy targets for more prominent financial services organisations or were liquidated.

Chaired by Stan Wallis (right), the Financial System Inquiry laid the groundwork for significant changes to the Australian financial services industry. Peter Morris/*The Sydney Morning Herald*

As Australia's largest friendly society, IOOF was relatively stable. However, taxation changes to the extended deeming rules for pensioners (in effect from 1 July 1996) contributed to a rush of funds from insurance and friendly society bonds as fund subscribers looked to exit their ten-year bonds. IOOF was not alone in its struggle to stem the flow and attract new funds.

Regulatory changes added to the uncertainty. The push towards more deregulation was boosted when the Liberal–National coalition led by John Howard won the federal election on 2 March 1996. Within three months of becoming federal treasurer, Peter Costello established a new Financial System Inquiry. Chaired by Stan Wallis, the inquiry was to make recommendations on the direction of the financial system:

~

The Inquiry is charged with providing a stocktake of the results arising from the financial deregulation of the Australian financial system since the early 1980s. The forces driving further change will be analysed, in particular, technological development. Recommendations will be made on the nature of the regulatory arrangements that will best ensure an efficient, responsive, competitive and flexible financial system to underpin stronger economic performance, consistent with financial stability, prudence, integrity and fairness.[1]

~

Another change afoot was in the state and national regulatory jurisdictions. In 1997, the Australian Financial Institutions Commission (AFIC) was set to assume oversight of the prudential standards of the sector, whilst state-based authorities would oversee the everyday activities of the friendly societies, enabling them to operate within a national framework. For most of their history, friendly societies had operated under state jurisdictions. Now, AFIC oversight meant friendly societies could become more national.

Just as Martyn Pickersgill had stepped into the top job in 1982 following the Campbell Inquiry's overhaul of the Australian economy, the person following Graham Cook would have to contend with a freshly conceptualised financial services industry. IOOF had adapted and prospered throughout the 1980s, taking advantage of the generally buoyant economy, but had hit a sticky patch in the early 1990s. Where would the Wallis Inquiry leave friendlies like IOOF? Could it compete with the leading financial services organisations?

Lindsay Bytheway knew corporate finance inside out, and he had been a member of the Grand United Independent Order of Odd Fellows in his younger days. Following time in Europe with Mayne Nickless, he had returned to Australia and focused on his family while looking to stay involved in the business world. That was how he had ended up at IOOF. Interviewed for this book, Bytheway said:

~

It was a lovely old society but was a story of the past, and was evidenced when we held AGMs, the members, the age grouping, their interests, what sort of activities they were involved in, and what they thought of IOOF. It was old-fashioned and quite different from a public company with financially invested shareholders. I'm sure the era was wonderful, but to my mind, coupled with the organisation's financial state, there needed to be many changes.

~

Despite his initial impressions, Bytheway could see the potential and the market opportunities. To realise that potential, Bytheway said, critical changes had to happen. Firstly, IOOF had to put the OST business to bed for good. Secondly, it needed a more professional and corporatised culture. Thirdly, it had to divest its non-core businesses and focus on its greatest emerging strength: funds management. Finally, it needed a leader to get everyone moving in the same direction. For all of this, a strategic plan had been developed by IOOF's executive team and endorsed by the board.

In early July 1996, IOOF announced it had appointed a new managing director, Robert Turner. Turner's most recent role was as executive director, executive interim management (Australia) of the Egon Zehnder Management Consulting Group. However, he had been on the IOOF board for three months, among the new faces brought in for the board's makeover. He officially took up his new position on 12 August 1996, with Cook continuing until then to ensure a smooth transition.

Bytheway knew of Turner mainly through his dealings with Egon Zehnder (Turner had helped place Cook with IOOF), but they also shared some interests and acquaintances. Lacking a background in the sector, Turner was a wildcard choice. 'Rob's appointment certainly wasn't based on his background experience in the industry,' Bytheway recalled.

~

In my whole working life, I've always acted on a gut feel, and I had a real gut feeling that Rob had the interest, desire, and energy to seize hold of the issue and go with it. Whereas many other people had looked at [IOOF] as somewhere to spend a few quiet years in an industry that would probably be alright and didn't need much attention, Rob was the opposite to that. He was very busy right from the outset. I had great confidence in him, and it was probably very fortuitous from my point of view that he was available at the time.

~

In many ways, IOOF was in stasis. The OST takeover, a flat economy and the move away from friendly societies by investors had all created a sense of lethargy. The diversification during the Pickersgill years also made the organisation feel disjointed. Cook steadied the organisation but did little to inject hope or optimism—which, in fairness, was not his brief.

Turner knew a little about the Australian finance industry when he started, but less about friendly societies. 'I knew about the Druids Health Fund because my in-laws . . . and my sister-in-law and family . . . were with the Druids, but that's all I knew,' he recalled in an interview for this book. 'It was a sharp learning curve, but I had people like Tony [Hodges], who was a guru in the industry, and I leaned on him a lot, and I picked up more and more as I went along,' he said.

The avid Richmond Tigers Football Club supporter soon warmed to the history of IOOF. He greatly respected its past and the work that friendly societies had done. 'I felt very supportive of the concept that when people didn't have government social support, the friendly societies did it. I came from not a well-off family, and no one in the family had ever been to the university before me. They were mainly tradespeople and other things.'

Turner's father had been a director at Richmond, and his grandfather a life member. While at IOOF, Turner was also on the board at Richmond. Now one of Melbourne's trendier inner-city suburbs, Richmond had been an industrial, working-class area. 'I could see the way the family had grown up,' he recalled. 'My mother's family, eight in the family in Richmond, struggled through the Depression. And I had a lot of empathy for the caring nature of the friendly society and the history.'

A Melbourne University accountancy graduate, Turner cut his teeth in the corporate world with adhesives giant Bostik, including two years at its global headquarters in Lausanne, Switzerland, and four years as a regional managing director. Before joining IOOF, Turner had compiled a diverse CV with an impressive array of companies, including Campbell's Soups, Collie Cooke and Egon Zehnder.

Turner had abundant enthusiasm and a charismatic leadership style that could galvanise a workforce. He was a people person. He could work a room but still have a hard conversation behind closed doors. Like Bytheway, he viewed the culture when he started at IOOF as lacking in rigour. 'I guess I brought strong corporate management experience and accountability to IOOF for the first time,' he recalled.

~

It was a mutual [society], and they were all doing a good thing for the members. But that culture had to change dramatically if they wanted to demutualise and ultimately list. And I was the change agent because I bought and sold companies in America and England and had that corporate experience.

We started a revolution in getting high-quality executives on board with full accountability, KPIs, short-term incentives, and reporting. I couldn't believe at the first board meeting, the reports to the board lacked critical details, and I had come from a corporate finance background. We changed the reporting so the board and the management were better informed. That was a significant change. We had to do these things to modernise the culture.

~

The 1996 annual report recorded that IOOF was far and away Australia's most successful friendly society, with 300,000 members.

It reported a group profit of $4.1 million for the 1995/96 financial year, a significant turnaround from the loss of a similar amount the previous year. Retained managed funds increased $4.1 million on the last year to $49 million, and funds under management totalled $3 billion. The main business groups were the friendly society; investments; retirement villages; building society; health insurance; financial planning; and trustee services.

It was a far cry from 150 years before, when William Clarke and his odd fellows first met at the Waterman's Arms. Over that century and a half, the organisation had endured many moments of doubt. Through the years, it had always pulled through for its members. But the demands of 1996 were a world away from 1846. The friendly society model was fit for purpose in 1846, but it now looked like a relic. The 1996 VicFIC annual report showed that total assets in the sector had declined again in the last year from $7.14 billion to $6.72 billion, with society numbers dropping from 89 to 82.

The following year, a damning report on the sector by the Institute of Actuaries of Australia stated: 'As fund managers, friendly societies are rapidly declining in importance in an expanding industry.'[2] IOOF had to adapt quickly. Bytheway and the board had a plan to make sure that happened. Turner believed he had the leadership skills to carry it out.

Federal Treasurer Peter Costello watched over the liberalisation of the financial services industry, which enabled businesses such as IOOF to expand into new markets for their products and services.
Michael Jones/Newspix

As Turner's tenure began, the OST saga showed signs of reaching closure. In July 1996, IOOF made discounted redemption offers to 31,000 policyholders in the failed OST Accumulator and Mortgage Bonds funds, worth $534 million in unlocked funds. Around 20,000 accepted the offers—those who did not were opting to hold their funds with IOOF. General Manager for Corporate Services Ross Higgins said in a newspaper report that it was a 'landmark step in the process of finalising the OST saga . . . We are delighted that investors have shown faith in IOOF's ability to manage their funds.'[3] In September, the slow-moving criminal case against two former OST directors, Bob Setterfield and Paul Allan Robinson, finally reached court. Setterfield, Robinson and two others were charged with fraud offences concerning loans authorised by OST.

IOOF diligently stuck to achieving the best possible result for OST investors, while integrating what was salvageable into its businesses. The takeover had sucked resources from the organisation and sapped morale. Bytheway said: 'They were difficult times for IOOF because they were more or less pressured, as I understood, to manage the [OST] funds. It distracted them considerably from establishing and growing their own business.'

At the start of 1997, the Malaysian-controlled company Quilter Assets Australia purchased Lasseters for nearly $20 million. (Quilter subsidiary Ford Dynasty would sell the hotel in 2021 for around $105 million.) The deal was completed after foreign investment and probity checks. Interviewed for this book, Tony Hodges outlined the strategy. 'We had two choices: liquidate or work the property out. If we had sold straight away, we would have only got a fraction of the price. It was a hard slog, but we wanted the best result for the OST investors.'

On 1 March 1997, the eagerly awaited Wallis Inquiry report was handed down. It set a blueprint for the financial services industry that accelerated the blurring of lines between banks and other financial services organisations. Labels like 'insurance company', 'credit union' or even 'friendly society' would diminish in importance as sector regulations were removed or folded into industry-wide mandates to enable businesses to compete across sectors.

The 39th recommendation of the report reinforced the transfer of friendly society regulation from state-based agencies to a federal authority, the Australian Financial Institutions Commission. The report's recommendations also established the 'twin peaks' of Australian financial services industry regulatory bodies, the Australian Prudential Regulation Authority (APRA) and the Australian Securities and Investments Commission (ASIC). Both were established on 1 July 1998 and designed to provide a streamlined national framework.

The report was good news for friendly societies, especially IOOF, which had sufficient funds, a sizeable member base and a strong brand reputation to stake out a spot in a highly deregulated financial marketplace. 'We could not have drafted or crafted that any better ourselves,' Turner said in a media interview following the report's release. 'The services we provide are much more aligned to what you would think a bank would be providing.'[4]

In the same interview, he heralded IOOF's new direction:

~

What I have tried to do is to build corporate values and a corporate vision into a mutual environment [to] make it a substantially more virile and growth-orientated organisation than it has been over the last few years. In the next six months, you will see some substantial innovative activity from IOOF.

~

Tellingly, the subject of demutualisation reared its head. However, Turner played his cards close to his chest. 'We see some considerable benefits in being a mutual and being such a closely focused member organisation,' he said.

Bytheway's recollection of the talk of demutualisation was that much of the interest was generated by journalistic speculation rather than any concrete plans, at least early on. 'It didn't come up for immediate discussion [with Turner]. It would have been some years before we got around to that. There were so many immediate problems to be attended to, putting out fires all around, so demutualisation was not high on the agenda,' he said.

The 1997 annual report showed promising signs that IOOF had turned the corner. Group profit after tax was $8.5 million; sales were up 40 per cent on the previous year; managed funds were at $57.7 million, up from $49 million; cash reserves were at $51.8 million, up from $28.4 million; and investment funds under management were sitting at around $3 billion. The problematic transitional years of the mid-1990s were giving way to encouraging growth, especially in the pivotal funds management area.

Turner's leadership had reinvigorated the organisation. At the start of 1998, IOOF reported a 120 per cent lift in funds management sales to $152 million for the six months to the end of December. More than 80 per cent of IOOF's revenue now came from sources such as master trusts and superannuation. Funds management and investments were booming. IOOF was making its intentions clear in the post-Wallis era. It was expanding its range of products and services, developing more complex products and platforms, and moving aggressively into retail and wholesale funds. The 'old-fashioned' friendly society on the brink of extinction a mere twenty years before was now squaring up to Macquarie, Bankers Trust and the Commonwealth Bank.

In April 1998, IOOF lifted the longstanding freeze on the OST Accumulator and mortgage bonds. More than 8500 investors with $55 million still in the funds could access the full value of their investments. Around $380 million had been paid out to OST investors since the 1990 freeze. IOOF had generated significant goodwill from OST investors, the friendly society sector and the financial services industry.

Speaking as president of the Australian Friendly Societies' Association, Martyn Pickersgill said the collapse of OST strengthened the non-banking financial sector and improved protection for investors. 'I don't think it [the Pyramid, Estate Mortgage and OST collapses] could happen again,' he said. 'The events of 1990 permeated the whole financial system, and everybody has since upped their standards . . . The system is so heavily tied to disclosure and prospectuses now it would be impossible.'[5]

The sense of relief within IOOF was palpable. Turner said to the *Australian Financial Review*: 'This is the end of the OST saga. We are most pleased the end has finally arrived. It has taken a lot of management time and resources, but there have been fantastic outcomes for the investors and IOOF.'[6]

The new millennium was met with optimism by many Australians, with a booming economy fuelling the growth of the wealth-management industry. Jim Rice/*The Sydney Morning Herald*

CHAPTER 11

TAKING FLIGHT

etirement villages had been core to the IOOF group's business plan during the Pickersgill era. By 1997, IOOF operated four: Cumberland View and Glendale in Melbourne; Riverwood in Albury; and Keperra Sanctuary in Brisbane. Group general manager of retirement care Casey Radcliffe had done an outstanding job since 1982 looking after the development of the villages. It was a worthwhile enterprise, winning awards for service and providing an excellent experience for residents.

However, the 1998 annual report signposted a radical pivot: 'We are currently seeking interest in the divestment of our retirement villages and, in doing so, are conscious of the need to ensure absolute certainty of tenure for the residents and a continuation of the high level of their care and comfort.'

Keperra Sanctuary was sold first, with Retirement by Design (a Delfin Property Group subsidiary) paying $7.75 million in May 1998. Late in 1998, Prime Life acquired the three other villages for around $20 million. The sale of the retirement villages ended a dream that had been fulfilled but that was no longer regarded as relevant to the business.

Bytheway said the retirement villages business held promise but was unsuitable for IOOF. 'I always thought that it would be a great opportunity, but it wasn't growing very quickly at that time,' he said. Time was precious. There was a strong belief that IOOF had fallen behind because of its OST commitments. To muscle up and compete as a funds manager, it had to sell assets that did not align with its primary goal and put aside sentimental attachments.

Selling the retirement business was a tough decision, because it spoke to the organisation's history and had been a significant achievement for the previous CEO, Martyn Pickersgill. Turner said: 'The chief executive fought long and hard for that. And that was probably one of my hardest decisions, along with the board, to face up to the members and let them know that we were departing.'

Exorcising OST and exiting the retirement business were springboards for the organisation to redefine its purpose. IOOF was not big enough to successfully be all things to all people. It had to pick a horse. Bytheway recalled:

~

The retirement villages, the building society, and the friendly society were all good businesses with prospects for the future, but we had to make up our minds about which ones, or which one, was going to be the most suitable for development and growth in the future, and we decided on funds management. The resources from the proceeds of the other businesses were pressed into that activity. It was not a particularly profound strategy. It was a progressive growth strategy with the need to clear the decks, getting rid of the problems, devoting more attention to the business that we saw as our principal operation.

~

In line with economic reforms and taxation changes, the household sector's balance sheet altered the financial system's shape. An increase in consumer holdings of market-linked investments and the declining share held in deposits led banks and other big financial services providers towards funds management. Regulatory changes meant non-bank financial institutions gained greater access to previously restricted markets. The increase in financial assets fostered the development of markets in a broader range of debt securities and investment products and a more critical role for institutional investors. IOOF's small but effective investment team had built its skills and reputation over the past decade. It was ready to step up. IOOF was knocking at the door to join the major funds management club.

The Howard government's neoliberalism, which embraced concepts like mutual obligation, reshaped the public discourse on social welfare and government intervention. The Coalition narrowly held on to power against the Kim Beazley–led Labor Party at the October 1998 federal election, losing the popular vote but coming out thirteen seats ahead. The liberal economic agenda encouraged the idea that individuals should be responsible for their own financial wellbeing, rather than the state.

In its 1996 annual report, IOOF encouraged this idea of self-sufficiency in keeping with the original friendly society ethos: 'IOOF was founded on the time-honoured principle of mutual self-help and we would urge the Government to implement appropriate measures to encourage individuals to save for financial independence especially in their retirement. Such measures should include the elimination of savings disincentives.'

Things had changed too radically in the post–World War II years for friendly societies to provide a safety net for working families again. But they could help families build wealth. The economy was growing again, and living standards were rising. The aspirations of the middle-class families and retirees who typically invested with IOOF were growing too.

Strong financial results throughout 1997 and 1998 buoyed the feeling that IOOF was on a sharp swing up from the early 1990s. Its retail sales figures more than doubled to $332 million between 1996/97 and 1997/98. Traditional tax-paid bonds sales lifted from $29 million to $46.5 million, and sales of trust products jumped from $95.5 million to $229.6 million. Providing a more comprehensive range of investment products, IOOF started to leverage its relationships in the independent financial-planning market. Adviser numbers grew at the wholly owned subsidiary Winchcombe Carson from 59 to 76. The various parts of the business were becoming better integrated.

A merry-go-round of mergers and acquisitions was in full swing as big and small entities attempted to determine where their strengths lay and how best to capitalise on them. IOOF's bid at the end of 1998 for the Stateguard Friendly Society, formed in the 1930s for State Bank of Victoria employees, was rejected. Missing out on the deal proved a minor setback. After some jostling between IOOF, the Commonwealth Bank and Australian Unity, the Stateguard board and members took their $440 million in funds under management to the South Australian financial group Lifeplan. (Lifeplan merged with Australian Unity in 2009.)

In March 1999, attention turned to a $20-million deal with Bendigo Bank. The regional Victorian bank acquired the IOOF Building Society under a cash/scrip offer, handing IOOF 3.7 million ordinary shares, equating to a 5.9 per cent stake in the bank. The deal involved a joint venture providing Bendigo Bank customers with funds management, advisory services and other forms of cooperation. It gave IOOF distribution channels for its products through the bank's branches, while giving Bendigo Bank access to IOOF's nearly 300,000 members. Seventeen IOOF building society branches were converted into Bendigo Bank branches.

Offloading the building society, established in 1988, continued IOOF's divestment strategy. Speaking to the *Australian Financial*

Review at the time, Turner was bullish about IOOF's direction: 'We're totally different to any other friendly societies. We're in the funds management business,' said Turner.[1]

Sue Herrald, who had worked in the IOOF Building Society, took up a client service role with high-net-worth customers after the sale to Bendigo Bank. She said Turner always had an open-door policy for anyone to come in and discuss the business. This created a convivial and collegiate atmosphere, she explained, easing her worries about the organisation's direction.

Interviewed for this book, she said the public was often confused by IOOF's array of businesses, which could make selling products and services challenging. 'We had already sold things like the travel agency by the time we sold the building society,' she noted. 'Most people perceived IOOF as a health insurer at the time. There were a lot of different entities. We were divesting because we were going towards pure funds management.'

The shape of the business was changing quickly, with momentum gathering towards a mooted demutualisation and public listing. On 1 July 1999, IOOF became a public company limited by shares and guarantees under the corporations law regulated by ASIC and APRA under the *Life Insurance Act* (1995). IOOF restructured as a group of companies limited by shares and guarantees, with the right to raise

IOOF entered into a successful joint venture with the Bendigo Bank to provide investment services to the regional bank's customers. Kelly Barnes/ AAP Image

share capital. This opened the door to more speculation about when demutualisation would happen. The official line from the 1999 annual report was coy:

~

We are often asked of our plans for demutualisation of the group. This matter is the subject of regular and serious analysis by the board. Whilst we are satisfied that our current mutual structure is presently more appropriate, we will continue to monitor developments and opportunities to maximise the strength of the group and to create wealth improvement opportunities for our members.

~

When Bytheway became chair in 1995, he set out to bring stronger corporate credentials to the organisation, including the board. The board of 1999 differed markedly from 1995, not least because two women, Dr Nora Scheinkestel and Kate Spargo, were now directors.

IOOF director Kate Spargo showed the changing face of the organisation as it moved towards a more diverse and inclusive culture. *Australian Financial Review*

Scheinkestel was a highly regarded lawyer and academic with expertise in project financing and business law. Spargo brought corporate governance and strategic insight to the table. The deputy chair, Roger Sexton, excelled in corporate restructures, mergers and acquisitions, and privatisation. Michael Parkinson brought experience from merchant banking and international investments. Ray Schoer provided regulatory and compliance expertise. Executive input came from Robert Turner. The solitary link to the old friendly society days was David Jury.

With more than 30 years of experience in investment banking and funds management, Mike Crivelli joined as a non-executive director in 1997 and became an executive director in August 1999. Crivelli was a funds-management industry star. He was among the first people Bankers Trust Australia founder Chris Corrigan had recruited, and made his name at the upstart firm. Crivelli left BT in 1996 to join Pacific Road Securities, a boutique international equities firm. His joining IOOF fitted the needs of the organisation.

'It was a continual process of getting knowledgeable people on the board and bringing something else with them as well and developing the business in different areas, like funds management,' Bytheway said.

Crivelli's involvement set the stage for IOOF's ascent in the funds-management industry. On 19 August 1999, IOOF Australia inked a joint venture with Crivelli and another funds industry heavyweight, Ian Macoun, to start the boutique firm Perennial Investment Partners Ltd (PIPL).

Tony Hodges remembered the day well because it was his birthday. 'We had Ian Macoun, the head of QIC [Queensland Investment Corporation], and Mike Crivelli,' he recalled.

~

So the three of us started PIPL. IOOF underwrote the deal, by contracting us to manage their funds, which was mainly fixed interest. It was about $3.7 billion, and that paid the rent, if you like. We leveraged off the existing IOOF investment division and added a few new professional investment managers and analysts who had more wholesale experience, and then took PIPL to the main asset management market through the asset consultants.

~

The PIPL board initially comprised Crivelli, Macoun, Hodges, Bytheway, Sexton and Turner. The joint venture was audacious. It required a leap of faith for many in the organisation and signalled a bold new direction.

Turner recalled unease among a few employees with the new arrangement, including details about remuneration for the PIPL directors:

~

Clearly, we couldn't match the salaries they were used to in the funds management industry. We gave a base salary, which was more than Tony and I were getting paid, but then they got equity. They came in on the basis of getting equity in the business, because salaries we couldn't even dream about were being paid by the likes of BT and Westpac.

~

Hodges explained that setting up Perennial required staffing and cultural adjustments:

~

We were doing things in IOOF that we needed to do that a boutique asset management company didn't want to do. We had issues about which staff went on which side. Did they go on IOOF? All the investment admin, all the investment performance reporting, did it go to Perennial's side? And the Perennial people wanted things to be very lean. There were issues with staffing and resources at the start. We lost a few staff.

~

Running a boutique funds-management firm required a cultural shift; the old friendlies culture did not always align with elite funds managers' mentality. 'We had some wonderful employees in IOOF that championed the members' interests. There was a bit of an "us and them" friction because we came from that grassroots level,' Hodges said. 'We aimed to create an environment where investment professionals could exceed their expectations. That's how we set it up.'

Speaking to the *Australian Financial Review*, Crivelli echoed Hodges about each partner's respective dowry: 'The big benefits we'll be getting through our association with IOOF is a very well-run, compliant and regulatory regime, which means that we will be able to leverage off that and put as much of our time, effort and resources as possible into actually managing funds.'[2] Another controlled entity, Perennial Value Management Limited, was incorporated in December 1999 as a funds-management company.

The Perennial venture garnered positive column inches in the financial media, bolstering the company's image. In the meantime, IOOF settled a long-running $60-million damages claim against the timber group Auspine. IOOF Australia Trustees had alleged Auspine had overcharged for harvesting expenses and not secured the best market prices for about 25,000 investors in a pine forest scheme. The unconditional settlement saw Auspine pay $12 million to IOOF covenant holders.

Another step into the new millennium was revamping the IOOF website, first launched in 1996. IOOF also worked overtime to ensure its IT infrastructure was Y2K compliant because of widespread concerns (unfounded in the end) that computer systems would crash when the date ticked over from 1999 to 2000. The company logo was redesigned, maintaining the traditional green and the interlinked double O at the heart of IOOF, but given a cleaner, more modern look. Along with the logo came the slogan 'Making Money Work', emphasising the new direction of the business.

The new company logo redesigned at the beginning of the new millennium created a cleaner, more modern look. Insignia Financial

The group was tracking well financially, and the divestment strategy reduced overheads while providing liquidity. IOOF was being refreshed for the new millennium and for its new direction. Indeed, it was about to undergo a radical rebirth at the turn of the 20th century. It would emerge as a completely new entity, while retaining its original essence.

The IOOF tower signage was a recognisable landmark on Collins Street, Melbourne. *Australian Financial Review*

CHAPTER 12

THE ROAD TO DEMUTUALISATION

Midway through 2000, IOOF moved into the 303 Collins Street development, at the corner of Collins and Elizabeth streets in Melbourne's CBD, leaving behind its head office at 22 St Kilda Road. The St Kilda Road headquarters was sold for $5.81 million, adding a little more to the organisation's war chest. The new address carried symbolic weight as the organisation sought to assert its place among the Collins Street financial elite. A 3500-square-metre lease earned IOOF naming rights on the 303 Collins Street building, with ground-floor retail space and levels 22, 23, 24 and 29 occupied by IOOF—the neon green IOOF sign on top of the building quickly became a city landmark.

Turner said the sign marked IOOF's arrival into new territory, figuratively and literally. 'We put the sign up. That was all about visibility and street credibility.' The new head office was near the old Waterman's Arms site on Little Collins Street, where the Duke of York Lodge members first met in 1846 to form the Independent Order of Odd Fellows.

He said the vogue among many financial institutions at that time was to shun history and embrace the new. Marketing gurus suggested a radical overhaul to the organisation's branding; Turner saw things differently and fought hard to keep the traditional green colour branding and references to the organisation's history. 'I wouldn't have a bar of losing the history. I told the marketing people that being established in 1846 sends a message that we are part of the fabric and history of this state and country.'

Despite radical changes over the previous five years, Turner said the organisation's mission to ensure members' financial wellbeing was always foremost. The prudent mentality that saw IOOF survive and prosper for over 150 years was still in evidence. 'In the funds management area, we weren't going to promote left-field concepts for investment. We were traditional people in equities and fixed interests, which was our in-house mentality.'

The structure of the organisation was almost unrecognisable from that in 1990. IOOF was getting lean and hungry. The divestment program continued apace. Around the time of the move to Collins Street in July 2000, IOOF sold IOOF Australia Trustees Ltd to the ASX-listed New Zealand financial services company Tower Ltd. IOOF director Roger Sexton said in a news report that 'the sale of

IOOF Trustees was always part of this strategy which is now nearing completion'.[1] IOOF could now more fully focus on funds management and financial services. The sale left IOOF with $3.8 billion of funds under management. 'Now we are back to where we want to be,' Turner told *The Australian* following the sale.[2]

The health insurance business remained, but it was a marginal concern. Funds management was starting to dwarf all else. The culture was starting to catch up with the structural changes, too. Bytheway initiated many of these changes as chair, including gradually revamping the board's composition. 'It was a progressive development,' he said. 'Each time we were short a board member, we looked at somebody perhaps more qualified.'

Recruiting people with specific high-level expertise to the board, such as Mike Crivelli, Michael Parkinson and Kate Spargo, enabled the organisation to run a ruler over its internal operations while expertly expanding into new areas. Bytheway said IOOF was also attracting fresh managerial and operational talent: 'New people came into positions like chief financial officer, investment officers, et cetera. People started to see it as a more attractive place to work. We began to see people with potential for future development coming to the organisation.'

Turner said the shift towards funds management required new skill sets: 'The older-style friendly society folk—without sounding cruel—were moved aside, and I brought in people from other corporations with a lot of power and experience in their particular categories.'

John Murray was a key recruit, joining in February 2000. The former head of Australian equities at Westpac Investment Management, Murray had worked at arguably the country's most successful boutique funds manager, Maple-Brown Abbott, and at Perpetual Funds Management. He was to head up a new value-based team of equity managers, Perennial Value Management, a subsidiary of PIPL.

Perennial hit the road running. By mid-2000, it was garnering positive feedback from the media, market and analysts. Five of IOOF's 31 retail open and closed funds achieved five-star ratings from Morningstar, a leading global investor research and ratings firm, an unprecedented result for IOOF after previously middling results. The buzz around Perennial was strong. Tony Hodges explained:

~

It was a perfect time to set up. Share prices had just dropped because the tech bubble had burst in March 2000, so we hit the share market running. The fixed-interest team worked well because it already managed a large pool of IOOF funds. So from a PIPL perspective, it was all institutional money. And down below, it became buckets of assets, that is Australian equities, global shares, fixed interest securities and cash, and where it came from up the tree, whether from retail or wholesale, it didn't matter. It just fell into buckets of assets that PIPL managed.

~

The Australian markets followed the US lead in dumping tech stocks. The dotcom bubble burst in March 2000, and the US NASDAQ fell by 75 per cent from March 2000 to October 2002. Analysts and investors were weary of the failed monetisation plans touted by ecommerce startups evangelising the world wide web. Companies such as Microsoft, Amazon, eBay, Qualcomm and Cisco survived to become giants in the digital economy, but many others disappeared.

IOOF and Perennial generally avoided exposure to tech stocks at the time, which meant few losses from the tech stock implosion. However, developing its in-house technology was a different matter. Dating back to the early 1980s overhaul of the organisation's IT infrastructure, IOOF had stayed abreast of digital solutions. By 2000, IOOF could count on a small but talented group of IT professionals to develop internal and external-facing solutions. The fruits of this commitment were products such as IOOF's Portfolio Management Service (MAX) and the internet-based Adviser DeskTop. MAX was a master fund and portfolio administration service, while Adviser DeskTop provided back-office support to advisers by providing up-to-date access to client accounts and unit price information.

IOOF began exploring sustainable, responsible and ethical investment as socially responsible investing became a more mainstream concern. It was a founding shareholder in what it described as Australia's first and only dedicated sustainable and socially responsible investment research group, the Sustainable Investment Research Institute (SIRIS). Founded by Mark Bytheway (Lindsay Bytheway's son) and with Charles Macek on its board, SIRIS was at the vanguard

IOOF partnered with the Sustainable Investment Research Institute to provide investors with more diverse ethical investment opportunities. Dylan Coker/Newspix

of the Australian sustainable and socially responsible investments sector. IOOF soon introduced its Socially Responsive Shares Fund, investing in companies that embraced socially responsible and sustainable performance in their corporate culture while offering strong returns.

In August 2000, David Jury retired from the board. Jury had served IOOF for 40 years, starting as a lodge official in 1960 and undertaking the chair's role during numerous stints, including the tumultuous years between 1991 and 1994. He was an ever-present and steady hand through good times and bad.

Ian Blair filled Jury's seat on the board. Appointed on 28 November 2000, Blair had previously been a director of IOOF Trustees Ltd. He brought a wealth of experience to the organisation from his long career with Deloitte Touche Tohmatsu, including five years as CEO. Turner said Blair's appointment typified Bytheway's push for more corporate talent on the board: 'He brought in people like Ian Blair and later Merran Kelsall, just two examples. These were high-calibre, high-level people.'

As 2001 progressed, IOOF was in excellent shape, settling into new offices and with the funds-management business growing strongly. Some in the media started to compare Perennial's performance to that of Maple-Brown Abbott. Bytheway helmed an experienced and talented board, while Turner oversaw a re-energised and optimistic management team and workforce. And then the sky darkened.

Sue Herrald has a clear memory of going to work the morning after 11 September 2001: 'Even though it wasn't directly financially related, September 11 changed a lot of things in the business. We had to do a lot of hand-holding with clients after that.'

September 11 was one of those 'before and after' days. Four hijacked planes in the United States crashed into either the ground or buildings, including the World Trade Center in New York, killing almost 3000 people. Witnessed by millions live on TV, those moments of terror shocked the world and ushered in an age of fear and uncertainty. Panic set in. Markets reacted swiftly.

US equity markets closed for four days following the attacks, its longest closure since the 1930s. It soon became apparent that this would be the most demanding investment environment since the 1987 crash. The preceding years had been shaky for international markets, with the Asian financial crisis in 1997, the Russian financial crisis in 1998 and then the dotcom crash in 2000. September 11 compounded the problems.

In the aftermath of September 11, Perennial adjusted course, reducing its cash holding sharply and raising its exposure to Australian industrial shares from 32 per cent of its portfolio to just over 38 per cent. It was keen to pick up undervalued stocks in the depressed market. It was a calculated risk but a wise move. Perennial stayed on course and performed well during a challenging period. Thankfully, the Australian economy did relatively well, being insulated from some of these international shocks.

On 18 October 2001, the IOOF board announced that it had approved a demutualisation plan, with members to vote on it by June 2002. Demutualisation would change IOOF's status from a mutual society to a shareholder company. 'The increased capital demands relating to growth and strategic initiatives make demutualisation the most appropriate option for restructuring our business,' Bytheway told *The Australian*. Also speaking to *The Australian*, Turner said the listing would aid capital raising: 'We have had terrific organic growth, but this will give us access to capital markets and speed up organic growth.'[3]

Since Pickersgill's tenure, finance journalists had raised the prospect of demutualisation, with IOOF usually responding with a polite no. It almost embarked on the process during the early 1990s, when it submitted a plan to the Insurance and Superannuation Commission. Discussions with potential backers stalled, and IOOF shelved the project.

This time, though, IOOF appeared ready. The organisation's shift towards funds management provided a firmer footing than its hydra-headed configuration of years gone by. Funds under management and advice now exceeded $4.7 billion. There were no travel agencies, retirement homes or Gold Coast theme parks to worry about. The board was well credentialled, with strong executive and operations talent driving the group's progress. But would the members agree to such a radical break from the past?

Turner recalled that the demutualisation push gained momentum following Perennial's establishment:

A member of the US military stands guard outside the New York Stock Exchange, September 2001. The global economy took a hit following the September 11 terror attacks as investors became nervous about geopolitical instability. John Feder/Newspix

~

I think we tossed it around, and we didn't bite the bullet for a while. Then we could see that there was value in this for the members, especially the older ones who had been members for decades. Also, to grow the business, it had to be listed on the stock exchange. It all evolved because we could see the growth opportunities in funds management. We could see that to get to the stock exchange listing; we would have to demutualise.

~

Bytheway said demutualisation was the next step in the organisation's evolution:

~

It was a compelling proposal. It would have happened by natural processes, as in other organisations. In some respects, we joined the queue, and it wasn't something that we thought about over many years. It wouldn't have been more than a year or two because we'd gone through the hiatus of 2000, and it was probably after that period that we started to think, where do we go from here? How can we grow this organisation? How can we change its structure? How can we obtain the necessary financial support we will need? So the steps moved to demutualisation, then public listing within some reasonable time afterwards.

~

IOOF presented an attractive proposal that involved returning more than $100 million in fund reserves to members in the form of shares. Eligible members were to receive a base share parcel valued at between $378 and $440, and then a further allocation of more than double that amount, with the exact number depending on the products they held and their length of membership. Demutualisation would release a windfall gain to members, in part tapping the accumulated value built by past generations. Hopes were high with a members' meeting and vote scheduled for 14 June 2002. But IOOF soon suffered a setback.

In mid-November 2002, Bytheway announced he was standing down as chair. The architect of IOOF's transformation cited personal reasons for retirement. 'I decided that if I were there for listing, I'd need to be there for some years afterwards because of the changes that would occur immediately following it,' he recalled. 'So I felt it better to go before as I couldn't continue for another three or four years.' He agreed to stay on until the vote.

Demutualisation in Australia happened in waves. Building societies and credit unions in the 1980s and early 1990s (such as the NSW Building Society, RESI/Statewide, Metway), life insurers in the 1990s (National Mutual, Colonial Mutual, AMP) and friendly societies in the early 2000s (the Over 50s Friendly Society and IOOF). In 2000, IOOF's old rival Australian Unity rejected persistent rumours it would demutualise. It again said no to demutualisation in 2005. Health insurers followed in the late 2000s.

The problems of insurance giant AMP cast doubt for some as to whether demutualisation was suitable for IOOF. AMP demutualised and listed in 1998, with $4 billion in surplus capital and no debt, but struggled after its international expansion plans failed. A further concern was the shaky stock market and a global economy still coming to grips with the shocks following September 11. Demutualisation also made IOOF attractive to bigger financial services organisations. 'That listing could make us a takeover target,' Turner told the *Australian Financial Review*. 'We do run that risk, and it's something the board of directors may have to deal with at the time.'[4]

The demutualisation announcement came on the back of more outstanding results for the organisation, which had reported a 45 per cent profit increase for the year to 30 June, from $5.57 million to $8.13 million. IOOF distributed $86 million in member bonuses and income distributions, up from $77.3 million the year before. The organisation also reported funds under management and administration exceeding $4.7 billion. In a raft of awards that year, IOOF Funds Management/Perennial Investment Partners was named Most Improved Fund Manager of the Year by Morningstar.

According to Turner, the solid performance and bright prospects of the group helped sell demutualisation to members:

~

It was well received by the members when they understood that they would still be shareholders in IOOF or could take cash or shares. So they weren't losing anything. Many were long-time investors in Tony's

[Hodges] fixed-interest and insurance bonds. That's where the main membership was, and they could see the benefits of demutualisation and listing. We didn't need to push it. We just put out the facts. There was certainly no major backlash against it.

~

Bytheway said once members understood they were getting a good deal, they were quickly on board: 'Demutualisation needed more explanation and elaboration to members on what it all meant and how it would affect them. When they learnt of the benefits, they came around very quickly.'

On 14 June 2002, at an extraordinary general meeting held at the Melbourne Concert Hall, Victorian Arts Centre, nearly 96 per cent of IOOF members supported a board recommendation to demutualise and become a public company. On 24 June, IOOF Ltd's plan to demutualise was given the green light by the Supreme Court of Victoria, with the process on schedule for completion by 30 June 2002.

In the 2002 annual report, Bytheway said: 'The year was a landmark one for the IOOF Group, highlighted by our members' support for the demutualisation proposal which changed our status from a mutual organisation to a shareholder-owned company.'

It was a fitting way to cap Bytheway's influential tenure as board chair. He had inherited an organisation searching for direction and was now departing as IOOF entered an exciting new phase of its 156-year journey, with plans for the company to list within a year.

According to Hodges, Bytheway's strategic thinking had always built on a nuanced grasp of operational details. 'Lindsay brought a commercial vision to the group,' said Hodges.

Turner was effusive about Bytheway's contribution:

~

He was the guiding light. When I got there, it was in Lindsay's mind, not so much the other directors who were wedded to the friendly society, but Lindsay could see that the days were numbered and we had to move into a singular field of expertise. It became increasingly evident to him, me and others that it was funds management.

~

Reflecting on his time, Bytheway said he enjoyed his tenure at IOOF: 'They were good people who were intent on making a success of the organisation, keeping it afloat, and that was achieved. It was part of the culture built into the organisation. That's a significant part of any business success.'

He was proud to play a crucial role in putting IOOF on the path to becoming a significant funds management business:

~

It was a considerable change from what I'd been doing most of my working life. I was also able, in many ways, to be actively involved in making changes in the organisation. I achieved great satisfaction from my time there.

I believe that if there was any contribution of any considerable extent on my part, then it was initiating the change that was necessary for the organisation's structure, its professional approach, how it dealt with external people, with its membership, and putting it in a position where it could be the organisation it is now, which I don't believe it could have been if it had continued in the way in which I found it in the early 1990s.

~

IOOF managing director Rob Turner (left) and chair Ray Schoer (right) were at the helm as IOOF successfully listed on the Australian Securities Exchange in December 2003. Paul Harris/*The Age*

CHAPTER 13

THE LISTING

F rom the *Geelong Advertiser* on Saturday, 18 July 1868:

~

ANCIENT INDEPENDENT ORDER OF ODD FELLOWS.

The sixth anniversary of the Winchelsea lodge of the A.I.O.O.F. was held yesterday. At 2 o'clock, the members, to the number of 55, assembled at the shire hall and marched in procession from thence, headed by Walker's brass band, through the principal streets of the township. The weather cleared up, and as the sun shone brightly, a number of friends joined in the procession. On their return to the shire hall, the brothers sang the opening ode when Grand Master William Stirling gave 'The Order.' He then called upon the secretary to read the report, which showed that the balance to the credit of the Lodge was £350 10s 7 1/2d. Brother Deputy Grand Sire A.J. Meacham then, in the presence of 200 ladies and gentlemen, commenced a lecture on the benefits accruing to those who joined the Order, which was listened to with great attention.[1]

~

On 14 June 2002, around 96 per cent of IOOF's 90,000 or so members voted to break with the past and embrace the future. It was as close to unanimous as possible for such a vote. Weighing up their choices and assessing their interests, IOOF members chose pragmatism. Demutualisation made sense to them and the business.

Still, it was hard to say farewell. But IOOF's history didn't disappear. It carried forth in a new form. Part of that DNA, an essential element of what kept IOOF alive for the past 156 years, was the company's resilience, its ability to adapt to circumstances, to reinvent itself and stay relevant. It had survived the Gold Rush of the 1850s. It had hung on during the economic strife of the 1890s, World War I, an influenza pandemic, the Great Depression and World War II. It had persisted throughout the expansion of the welfare state in the post-war years. Now it was taking its first steps towards becoming a publicly listed company.

Robert Turner was emphatic about the organisation's direction but proud of its history. He did not view the past as an encumbrance. 'I like to hang onto it a bit,' he said. 'It means something. When we moved into the new offices, they wanted to toss some old stuff like the Grand Master's chair. I put it in the foyer upstairs. I made sure we had some of the regalia installed there.'

However, history is more than memorabilia. It lives on through people and culture, informing how an organisation operates. It is the bedrock of corporate memory.

Sharon Savannah (nee Fernandesz) joined IOOF full-time in 2000 after working extensively with mutuals, investment and other insurance providers. Before joining IOOF, she consulted to the organisation while on maternity leave. She was impressed by its ambition to move into funds management on a grander scale, which encouraged her to take a full-time position in the high-net-worth wealth-management unit.

Currently the Head of Investment Funds within Asset Management for Insignia Financial, Savannah recalled that the switch from mutual to shareholder-owned company, while an exciting time, presented challenges for staff, many of whom had spent their formative years within the friendly society:

~

There were probably mixed emotions given the significant change at the time. There were undoubtedly benefits from a business growth perspective, but looking more from the staff culture lens, many of the core people working at IOOF had been there a long time and imbedded in its private member-owned culture. Demutualisation introduced a shift in that mentality and focus. Moving to a listed company created a greater emphasis on the shareholder, capital and public positioning—a change which was not initially comfortable for all.

~

Following demutualisation, IOOF busily prepared for public listing on the ASX. Lindsay Bytheway stayed chair until the close of the 2002 annual general meeting, officially retiring as a director on 17 December 2002, after ten years on the board and seven as chair.

IOOF was in good hands, with Dr Roger Sexton as deputy chair, alongside highly experienced heads such as Ian Blair, Michael Parkinson and Charles Macek, who took over the chair from Bytheway on 20 August 2002. Macek, a Czechoslovakia-born refugee, had spent his executive career in financial services, principally asset management. Like Turner, Macek barracked for the Richmond Tigers and was a club board member.

One concern for the board was that several larger firms were rumoured to be sizing up IOOF as a takeover target. To this end, the company included a shareholding cap of 10 per cent for the first five years in its new constitution. In early August 2002, Bendigo Bank acquired around 8.5 per cent, or 4 million shares, in IOOF Holdings Ltd, with an offer price of $2.70 per share to shareholders. Earlier, IOOF sold its 50 per cent interest in Bendigo Investment Services to Bendigo Bank as part of a broader alliance, which involved providing funds management administration and investment management services. The Bendigo Bank holding consolidated the partnership between the regional bank and IOOF, forged through previous joint holdings and ventures, and gave IOOF some insurance against a hostile takeover.

The year after the September 11 attacks proved challenging for investors, with negative returns experienced by both international and domestic share markets. The global war on terror, the continued deflation of the tech bubble and company collapses in the United

The September 11 attack and resulting Iraq War cast a long shadow across the economy and financial markets. Robert H. Baumgartner/Wikimedia Commons

States negatively affected investor sentiment and share-market performance worldwide.

Nervousness crept into the timing of the listing. In a newspaper report in November 2002, Turner said: 'Our assessment of the market is that it is probably not the best time to be going into the market [but] we are very aware of our members and their need to be able to sell their shares.' He said in the same report that acquisitions were on the horizon: 'Given the consolidation that's going on in the industry at the moment . . . we are certainly out there looking for opportunities for acquisitions to increase our scale.' He also talked up IOOF's aspirations to break into the ASX 200. 'If we deliver on our plans over the next couple of years organically, then we believe we'll get ourselves into that category,' he said. 'If institutions are going to take any notice of us then of course we have to be in the top 200.'[2]

Despite the economic chill, IOOF continued to perform well, led by Perennial's strong showing. The group's business units performed very well, with sales increasing to $1.5 billion, up from $800 million in the previous year. Over the same period, net profit rose to $15.6 million, up from $8.1 million. Group funds under management and administration increased to $3.9 billion on 30 June 2002.

Winchcombe Carson Financial Planning continued its growth, with $1.7 billion in funds under advice. Further development in financial planning was underpinned by expanding IOOF's financial advice network with the Australian Financial Planning Network (AFPN) launch. AFPN provided back-office support for Winchcombe Carson and other financial planning firms where IOOF held equity interest.

Turner announced in February 2003 that IOOF would delay listing because of market uncertainty arising from the prospect of a war in the Middle East and a flagging US economy. 'We do not believe that now is the right time to be going to the market,' he told the *Herald Sun*.[3] On 20 March 2003, the United States invaded Iraq. Virgin Blue, Cashcard, Repco, Pacific Brands, JB Hi-Fi, Just Jeans and Invocare were among the other businesses that also put a listing on hold that year.

Meanwhile, IOOF added significantly to its stake in the burgeoning superannuation sector, acquiring some of the superannuation and investment specialist AM Corporation's businesses. The acquisition added $5 billion in funds under management to IOOF overnight. AM was engaged in a stoush with MLC and began to attract the unwanted attention of regulators. AM's directors would face further problems the following year, none of which affected IOOF, which did not formally acquire the trustee company or AM itself, just the businesses they ran.

Turner said the acquisition boosted funds under management but presented integration challenges. 'It took a couple of years to bed down the AM business because we reduced the staff by 150,' he explained. 'We had to integrate some of their people into our business, which doesn't always happen easily, and we let some go.'

IOOF also let go of its health fund—the final divestment of its legacy businesses. From the very start, IOOF had provided health coverage in some form or another. Health funds developed throughout the 1800s and into the early 1900s until the doctors' dispute of the late 1910s diminished the societies' bargaining power. The healthcare insurance landscape changed considerably in the post-war years. IOOF maintained its health business throughout all this, but subscriber numbers dwindled, as did the size of the business.

NIB acquired the health insurance business for around $13 million, with IOOF making a $7-million profit on the sale. Turner said the health fund was well run but struggled to compete with the big players like BUPA. 'The health fund suffered because you need large capital resources on the balance sheet for a fund, and we didn't have that,' he noted.

The sale of IOOF's health fund to NIB in March 2003 completed a divestment program that saw IOOF pivot to wealth management.
SOPA Images/Alamy

The IOOF Health Services sale completed the non-core divestment program. In a nod to history, Turner entertained long-time members Nell Meneilly and her friend Muriel Spencer, whose combined IOOF memberships spanned 99 years, at an event marking IOOF's exit from the health funds business. (Nell Meneilly was the widow of Jim Meneilly, a key figure in the history of IOOF.)

On 19 August 2003, IOOF chair Charles Macek resigned, citing other commitments, including chairing the Financial Reporting Council. His departure as chair marked the beginning of a period during which several other vital figures exited.

Ray Schoer, a non-executive director of IOOF since 1994, was appointed to replace Macek. From 1990 to 1995, he was the national director of the Australian Stock Exchange Ltd, and from 1980 to 1990, he was chief executive officer of the National Companies and Securities Commission. He knew the business well, and his regulatory and governance background was suited to the upcoming challenges.

Turner recalled that it was a testing time for the organisation internally. The protracted preparations for listing, the health business sale and the AM acquisition were all agenda items. Implementing the *Financial Services Reform Act*, which was initiated as a result of the Wallis Inquiry, was also a pressing task and would continue to significantly impact the financial planning industry and market conditions.

Less than two weeks after Macek departed, PIPL managing director Ian Macoun resigned. Macoun was a fundamental part of the Perennial business and one of the founding directors. Perennial was changing its ownership structure and becoming a more independent entity. It established an autonomous board but retained IOOF as a major shareholder and financial backer. Since 2000, Perennial's funds under management had grown from $2 billion to $5.5 billion, during which time many other rival funds managers struggled. It was also named Fund Manager of the Year in 2002 by Morningstar.

Financially, IOOF was in good shape. It posted a net profit of $34 million for the 2002/03 year. The result doubled the previous year's profit of $16 million, and the business enjoyed a 32 per cent lift in revenue to $160 million. The AM acquisitions had significantly boosted funds under management. In the past twelve months, IOOF won mandates to manage the Optus and Flight Centre superannuation accounts. It had a strong balance sheet with no debt and was looking at acquisitions. It was beginning to achieve the critical mass required to compete with the big life insurers and banks dominating the funds management industry. But there were troubling signs of ruction within the board and executive. Rumours circulated that IOOF was an acquisition target for Perpetual Investments.

On 17 October 2003, IOOF issued its prospectus, outlining a plan to list in early December and raise around $40 million by selling 13.3 million shares at $3.15 per share. Current stakeholders were offered a minimum of $1000 in shares, but a substantial amount was offered to institutions in a book build undertaken by Goldman Sachs JBWere. The estimated market capitalisation was around $200 million.

However, a note of caution stuck out in the prospectus regarding discussions with senior executives of PIPL and Perennial Value Management: 'If the parties cannot reach agreement in relation to a revised shareholders agreement, one or more executives of Perennial Value Management Ltd may depart.' Among the senior executives concerned was John Murray, the former head of Australian equities at Westpac Investment Management and a key figure for Perennial Value Management Ltd.

On 24 October 2003, IOOF dropped a bombshell: it was not renewing Turner's five-year contract, which was due to expire the following June. The statement thanked Turner for his work but did not expand on the reasons for its decision. 'Together with the board, Rob has overseen the successful sale and divestment of non-core assets such as our retirement villages and health fund, the establishment of the highly successful boutique funds management business, Perennial, and this year the acquisition of the Sydney-based AM Corporation,' Schoer said in a media statement. Turner would work with the board to find a replacement and continued to support the listing in December. A staff memo was no more forthcoming with details.

Since demutualisation, IOOF had seen the departure of two chairmen, the managing director of PIPL and now its long-serving and popular CEO. There were also rumours that a star funds manager would be leaving. The wheels started looking wobbly as IOOF approached the listing.

In early November 2003, IOOF Holdings Ltd applied for admission to the Official List of the ASX and was allocated the listing code IFL. The company AGM was scheduled for 20 November, and the listing date for 5 December.

Turner's upcoming exit was poorly received by some. He was popular with members and had cultivated a strong relationship with the financial planning community.

The AGM was a fiery affair, the AAP reported. One member called for a vote on Turner's contract renewal. Numerous financial planners warned of an exodus of planners and funds if it replaced Turner. 'The funds under management you have today will be gone tomorrow if you get up the noses of the non-aligned financial planners,' one financial planner said.

Responding to the protests, Schoer said: 'We see shareholders would be better served by recruiting someone with extensive experience in the [funds management] industry. IOOF is more than one person. If he [Turner] is not there, the sky will not fall in.' Some members jeered Schoer. Turner responded: 'I am but one person in this organisation. We have capable staff who will provide service.'[4]

Two weeks out from the listing, the AGM did not inspire confidence. Attempting to quell the situation, Turner told the media:

~

The fact that I am going once a suitable replacement is found in no way diminishes the capabilities of the group in the lead-up to its listing and beyond. I would expect the management team to continue to build on the strategy we, as a group, have conceived and developed.[5]

~

Interviewed for this book, Turner reflected on the episode and said the decision hurt him. But he did not want to jeopardise the hard work that he, Bytheway and Tony Hodges, the Head of Strategy, had put in. 'Everybody was pushing towards the listing, and we perhaps had different ways of doing it, but we came to a common methodology and we were well advised by JBWere,' he recalled. 'The board wanted a fresh set of eyes, which was their prerogative of course.'

The book build was completed days before the listing. Some, including the *Australian Financial Review*'s Chanticleer, viewed IOOF's chances of success with scepticism:

~

Today a small Melbourne-based company will list with a relatively new chairman, the former National Companies and Securities Commission power broker Ray Schoer, whose time in the job would seem to be limited . . . From an outside perspective IOOF has every appearance of a disaster waiting to happen, with more questions than answers, which is no time for Schoer and his board to have their hands out looking for funds.[6]

~

IOOF company secretary Mary Latham sent a fax to the ASX Melbourne Listings Department on 4 December outlining the details of the listing, including that:

- The prospectus offer dated 17 October 2003 closed at 5 pm on Monday, 1 December 2003.
- The company received and accepted valid applications for 29,375,584 ordinary shares fully paid at a sale price of $3.15 per share.
- The company had an appropriate spread of shareholders and at least 500 shareholders, each having a parcel of ordinary shares with a value of at least $2000.
- The final number of fully paid shares to be quoted was 63,435,547.

The last point under information for release to the market: 'We confirm that the company has decided not to renew the existing Managing Director's employment contract.'

Defying the naysayers, IOOF successfully listed and raised $41.89 million. Bendigo Bank was the largest shareholder, with 9.4 per cent. On 6 December, IOOF started trading at $3.80 and closed at $3.96.

Turner said the result did not surprise him. He reflected that he and his team had worked around the clock, with numerous road trips and relationship-building excursions to Sydney-based asset managers. 'We were seen as an attractive stock, and some of the investment houses did take meaningful shares at the listing,' he said.

Turner had joined IOOF midway through 1996, when it was directionless and in a leadership vacuum. He oversaw its most significant transformation, from a friendly society to a listed company.

His leadership enabled the organisation to re-energise and find a new purpose.

Looking back, he said his tenure at IOOF was a special time in his professional life, filled with wonderful people, considerable challenges and excellent outcomes. 'We had to conduct a revolution,' he recalled. 'In people on the board, the management staff and the whole understanding of what the future held and what the past wouldn't deliver in those business units. So when I left, it was a funds management business with tremendous momentum.'

IOOF chief executive Ron Dewhurst was highly regarded for his talent
management and deep knowledge of global investment banking.
Colin Murty/Newspix

CHAPTER 14

GROWING UP
IN PUBLIC

✻

Adrianna Bisogni joined IOOF in 2003 as general counsel from Rothschild Asset Management Ltd. She recalled that Robert Turner interviewed her for the job, and that the organisation was preparing to list. She knew of the organisation's history as a friendly society but was unprepared for what awaited her when she started.

In an interview for this book, Bisogni said: 'I barely left my office in that first year. I'd sit there from 7.30 in the morning till about six at night. I would be lucky if I could get a sandwich.'

The deputy chair at the time, Roger Sexton, recalled that the period between demutualisation and listing was a blur of activity to ensure IOOF could fulfil its regulatory obligations and market demands:

~

I think it was taking the culture of the organisation, which was pretty much like a family company, to a company that was going to be in the public sphere with all the normal governance and regulatory controls that go with that, audit committees and compliance committees, and putting all that in place, and changing the culture.

~

Having this high-level strategy in place to become a public company was one thing, but fulfilling that aspiration required heavy lifting. Employees like Bisogni undertook the grunt of transforming a friendly society into a public company. IOOF listed at the start of December 2003. Turner was still CEO, but his tenure was effectively over. Chair Ray Schoer was looking for a fresh face to lead the organisation, but the search was proving difficult. Rumours circulated about prospective hires, including former AMP boss Paul Batchelor, but the clock was ticking.

Despite the leadership vacuum, the listing was well received, and IOOF continued to attract positive investor sentiment, trading well above its issue price of $3.15. The share price continued to perform well over the next few months, reflecting the modest price at which the public issue had been placed and the industry's overall attractiveness.

Another concern before the listing was Perennial. The retention of John Murray, an integral talent for Perennial Value Management, was raised in the listing prospectus and hung over the business as it searched for a new CEO. In February 2004, Schoer announced a revenue-sharing deal with Murray and the other Perennial executives. He told the *Australian Financial Review* that the agreement meant Perennial would retain Murray's services for some years: 'It's to remove any doubt about the future of Perennial.'[1]

Under Bytheway, the board identified funds management as the future of IOOF. That did not change with Schoer, and the board wanted to find someone with the experience to take IOOF to the next level as a funds manager.

In March 2004, IOOF appointed Ron Dewhurst as managing director. Before joining IOOF, he was Head of Americas for JP Morgan Asset Management, a business with $800 billion in assets. By comparison, IOOF had around $13.8 billion in funds under management and administration. Dewhurst was an impressive catch. He had started his finance career with Melbourne stockbroking firm McCaughan Dyson. He became the CEO of ANZ McCaughan in 1990. In 1992, he joined JP Morgan, running the Asian and European equities divisions before moving to JP Morgan Asset Management.

Dewhurst had made a successful life for himself and his family overseas. However, towards the end of 2002, his father-in-law was gravely ill, which brought him back to his hometown, Melbourne, and to IOOF.

Interviewed for this book, Dewhurst said he was effectively in retirement when IOOF came calling:

~

They had recently demutualised and become a public company, and the board had come to the view that things weren't going as well as they hoped. They were dealing with the pains of moving from a mutual to a public company. So I was asked if I'd be interested in taking on the CEO role.

~

Hiring Dewhurst was a coup. He was highly accomplished on the global funds management scene and admired for his achievements on

John Murray joined in February 2000 to head up Perennial Value Management, a subsidiary of IOOF. Perennial was vital to IOOF's growth in the 2000s. Matthew Vasilescu/Newspix

Wall Street. He was also an elite-level athletics coach, having guided the legendary Australian runner Raelene Boyle to a Commonwealth Games gold medal in 1982. Dewhurst knew funds management inside out and was an excellent people manager, drawing on his work with athletes to get the best from his employees.

Speaking later in the year at the company AGM, Schoer expressed his relief at landing Dewhurst's signature. 'It's a very painful experience trying to recruit a good CEO, and Mr Dewhurst at that stage was sought by other people, and has been sought by other people since,' he said.

According to Dewhurst, his skills would first be tested in dealing with a dichotomous culture within IOOF. 'There was this tension between the traditional business, what IOOF had been, and this new developing business, Perennial, which was growing at a clip,' said Dewhurst. 'When I arrived at IOOF, the relationship between Perennial and the company's management was poor.'

Dewhurst set about building bridges between the two camps:

~

One of the things you need to do when you run an asset management business is to make sure you recognise the intellectual capital that drives the investment performance. Those people are a little bit like champion athletes. They don't all necessarily come in an easy-to-manage form. They each come with their own challenges and foibles.

~

Dewhurst's appointment was an immediate tonic for the share price. By July 2004, IOOF shares surged to $5.15, making the company the second-best performer among new listings in the previous twelve months. Earnings for 2003/2004 were expected to be 20 per cent to 30 per cent higher than prospectus forecasts. Funds under management and administration would hit around $16 billion, well ahead of the prospectus forecast of $13.8 billion.

Along with the positive bottom line results came speculation about takeovers and mergers, with Colonial First State, Peter Morgan's 452 Capital, Bendigo Bank, St George Bank and Perpetual Trustees rumoured as suitors. But the speculation was no more than that, because of the 10 per cent shareholding cap. While not making a takeover impossible, it raised the hurdle high. Still, the rumours put IOOF employees on edge.

Dewhurst was aware of his challenges in moving the company towards a new horizon. 'I don't want us to appear on the one hand to have gone from a caring, sharing organisation that wasn't particularly profit motivated to a firm that only wants to worry about its profit margin,' he told a media briefing. 'We're not the company we used to be, and we're not the company we want to be yet.'[2]

To this end, Dewhurst realised the importance of utilising his resources. In Tony Hodges, he identified someone who could help unify the old and new factions of the business. In September 2004, Hodges was appointed to the board as an executive director, while also serving as the executive director of several group subsidiaries including Perennial Investment Partners Ltd, Perennial Investment Partners Asia Ltd and Perennial Value Management Ltd.

Dewhurst said Hodges always had the business's best interests at heart. 'He was the bedrock of the place,' he explained. 'The father confessor. He had a good understanding of the business and perhaps had not always been listened to as much as he should have been. I don't know that for a fact, but that was my instinct.'

However, Dewhurst said it was sometimes difficult to escape some of the more mundane friendly society baggage, as this newspaper report shows:

~

New boss Ron Dewhurst told an investor briefing yesterday that it still gets some rather strange inquiries. Apparently, someone rang up the other day asking if the company could suggest a suitable person to fix a broken fridge. We gather the old friendly societies used to provide such services. But it is not one of its core competencies these days.[3]

~

The quirky report indicated that the newly listed business still struggled with its brand identity. For the general public, IOOF was variously seen as an insurance office, health fund provider, super fund or building society. In the financial services community, it was desperately trying to consolidate its credentials as a funds manager of national standing.

Dewhurst understood that many still viewed the company as a jack of all trades, rather than as a specialist funds manager. 'It needed to establish a persona,' he said. 'It was a matter of changing gears without hurting the good parts of the organisation and still fostering the ethos and the values the company aspired to.'

Maria Bonham-Gilberd joined IOOF in 2005 and worked on various projects, including the development of what was a flagship platform product, IOOF Pursuit, which launched in 2006. She remembered it was a fast-paced and sometimes frustrating time. 'There were so many competing priorities, but there was also a considerable amount of change happening that added to the challenges,' she said.

When interviewed, long-time employee Sharon Savannah recalled that it was an uncertain period for the business: 'There was still a tug-of-war in terms of who we were. Are we doing funds management, asset management, or are we going to focus on super platform management? Plus we had the friendly society business on the side.'

The bigger economic picture looked bright. The market was experiencing an uplift after the trough of the early 2000s, and funds were pouring into superannuation, helped by federal government initiatives. The AM Corporation acquisitions were finalised, increasing IOOF's exposure to the superannuation market. The general investment climate was improving, and the Australian economy, bolstered by the beginnings of the mining boom around 2003, was also in better shape than many international counterparts. The federal election held on 9 October 2004 saw the return of John Howard's Coalition government.

In Dewhurst's first six months, he thoroughly reviewed the strategy for the business. Unlike the radical surgery performed under Bytheway and Turner, Dewhurst and the board decided there was no need to do anything remarkably different. Instead, IOOF had to back its strengths and sharpen its focus. Developing cohesion between IOOF and the Perennial business was crucial.

The relationship between IOOF and Perennial was becoming a headache for Dewhurst. The previous year, Perennial founder Ian Macoun had left the business. Now another founding partner, Kerry Series, was going. Series was a critical figure in international equities, and his departure in September was met with murmurs of disapproval by market analysts.

Dewhurst had to create a sense of unity and shared purpose for IOOF to continue growing as a funds manager. He said a balance had to be struck:

~

A business should have dynamic tension because that's good for business. When it declines to being adversarial, and there was an element of hostility there, that's not good. And one of the things management can be inclined to do in a situation like that is to resort to an attitude of: 'Do you realise who I am? I'm the boss.' That doesn't necessarily win the hearts and minds of the people you're trying to keep in the business, who are the talents. There has to be mutual respect there.

~

At the end of 2004, Dewhurst laid out a plan for closer distribution alliances, new products and better service levels. Speaking to

The Australian, he said IOOF would not rely on acquisitions to achieve growth and warned that some measures would not yield immediate results. 'Acquisitions are of interest to us, but we are not reliant on them to execute our strategy,' he said.[4]

IOOF focused on advice, platforms and active funds management through its alliance with Perennial Investments. By year's end, it had a market capitalisation of $500.51 million, making it the 148th largest company in the SP/ASX 200 index.

The following year was stable. Mark Blackburn became the new chief financial officer, replacing the long-serving Alan Mollison. Results for the 2004/05 financial year were positive, with net profit increasing by 58 per cent to $65.1 million, after-tax profit at $18.3 million and cash earnings increasing by 86 per cent to $34.9 million. Total assets under management grew from $15.9 billion to $22.4 billion, a 41 per cent increase.

The growing pains of a newly listed company had eased, with a focus on rolling out new products and services. Interestingly, Dewhurst signalled turbulence ahead for the market. Speaking to the *Australian Financial Review* in September 2005, he said: 'My view is it's getting harder to find places to get money to work . . . I'm not talking the market down, but realistically I think we've been through a halcyon period in the markets.'[5]

On 15 November 2005, Schoer ended his tenure as chair, with Ian Blair taking over. Blair had been a non-executive director of IOOF Holdings Ltd since 2002 and a non-executive director of IOOF Ltd from 2000 to 2002. A chartered accountant and company director, he was a safe pair of hands for the organisation as it settled into life as a listed company.

The beginning of 2006 was more notable for the activities of IOOF's competition. Funds management businesses, always looking for scalable opportunities, were once more on the mergers-and-acquisitions (M&A) merry-go-round. Rationalisation, consolidation and scale were the keywords thrown around by analysts. Significantly, Australian Wealth Management (AWM) and Select Managed Funds merged, creating an entity with a market capitalisation of around $840 million and funds under management, administration and advice of $22 billion. The combined market cap made it almost double the size of IOOF. Both companies were already undertaking M&A activity, with AWM recently acquiring ABN Amro's two corporate trust businesses. Select, a superannuation, administration and funds

Client file storage cabinets, like these ones in the basement of the MLC building in Miller Street, North Sydney (a business IOOF purchased in May 2021), were consigned to history as finance businesses embraced computerisation and digital technologies. Insignia Financial

management specialist, made several small acquisitions, including the Merrill Lynch Super and Pension Fund.

IOOF was wary of being muscled out of the funds management game. Its advances towards wholesale investment administration group Oasis Asset Management, with $3 billion under administration, were rebuffed. ING Australia paid $54 million for a 76 per cent stake in Oasis Asset Management. Insurance giant Aviva also expressed interest in Oasis.

Meanwhile, IOOF agreed to buy 75 per cent of the Financial Partnership advisory business—one of Australia's first lifestyle financial planning groups—it did not own in cash and stock. The plan was to merge Financial Partnership with Winchcombe Carson to grow the financial planning and advice business. The new group became Consultum Financial Advisers in 2006.

The 2005/06 financial year results were again healthy. Funds under management and administration approached $29 billion, a 29 per cent growth rate on the previous year. Net profit was up 54 per cent to $23 million. The group's cash earnings rose 40 per cent to $44 million. Momentum was building, and Dewhurst's vision of a more focused and unified business was taking shape.

Then, in October 2006, the shape of the business again changed dramatically. IOOF paid $67.9 million to buy the 21.85 per cent of shares it didn't own in Perennial Investment Partners to take complete control of the firm. Perennial was coming in-house. Perennial executive chair Michael Crivelli was paid an initial $15 million for his shares, while managing director Anthony Patterson received $26.6 million for his parcel. The two were slated to receive deferred payments when Perennial reached performance targets in 2008/09.

Dewhurst told the *Australian Financial Review*: 'The market loves instant gratification these days, but this is a strategic long-term play for us in how we build the business long term.' Some analysts were sceptical about the price paid for Perennial. But Dewhurst was convinced it was a good deal, telling the *Australian Financial Review*: 'This purchase: we had our eyes wide open. We believe in the sector long term.'[6]

In January 2007, Dewhurst resigned. His decision surprised many, but he told *The Australian* he had achieved his aims:

~

I think the company is at an inflection point right now, which requires another three-year commitment from the CEO, which I don't feel I want to do. There's been no fallout with the board. I'm not unhappy with the company. I just think it's the right time for me to make this decision.[7]

~

Interviewed for this book, Dewhurst said he always saw his role as finite, helping IOOF transition into its new status as a publicly listed company. After three years, he was ready for a new challenge:

~

My experience, fundamentally, was much more international, and IOOF was purely domestic. There was a limit to my interest level in the asset management business being a domestic-only business. I'd been there for three years and did what I needed to do to help the company. I enjoyed my time there. I enjoyed the management team I had around me. They worked hard. There was a good sense of community and great care for the organisation.

~

The rise of hedge funds, short selling and computerised trading created new complexity in financial markets. Peter Braig/*Australian Financial Review*

CHAPTER 15

MERGERS, ACQUISITIONS AND THE GFC

The modernisation of the Australian financial services industry began with the 1981 Campbell Committee inquiry. It drew a line in the sand between the previous decades of interventionist regulation and a more market-based outlook that encouraged competition and choice for consumers.

The 1997 Wallis Inquiry report reviewed and updated the Campbell reforms. It freed financial services businesses from their sector silos, enabling them to move more easily between traditionally demarcated products and services, increasing competition and choice.

However, the modern financial services landscape was also shaped by a policy that sought to maintain the system's stability by sanctifying the position of the four biggest banks—ANZ, the Commonwealth Bank, NAB and Westpac—as large and independent competitors to each other. The initial iteration of the policy, outlined by Paul Keating, involved 'six pillars', which included the Big Four banks plus the two most prominent insurance offices, AMP and National Mutual Life.

The pillars policy prohibited mergers between the Big Four banks and the two life insurers. Keating had announced the policy in the wake of the proposed merger in 1990 between ANZ and National Mutual. He stated that the union 'would be contrary to the national interest and should not proceed'.

He continued:

~

Australia would be served better by banks and other financial institutions interested in obtaining a larger share of superannuation and life insurance business continuing to grow their own operations, rather than seeking to acquire size by taking over large life insurance companies. Equally, it would be preferable for life companies that wish to expand into banking to grow organically or by acquiring relatively smaller institutions. At the present level of competition, it would be preferable for the six or seven largest institutions in these industries to remain separate . . . The Government must judge whether the normal freedom of commercial operators needs to be restricted in the broader national interest.[1]

~

The pillars policy attracted bipartisan political support despite criticisms that it was anti-competitive and would stifle innovation. The Wallis Inquiry had argued for abandoning it, but the Howard government rejected that view. However, the policy soon lost two of its pillars when treasurer Peter Costello allowed the banks scope to merge with or acquire the big insurance offices.

The policy continued to influence mergers and acquisitions throughout the 1990s and 2000s, with the big banks seeking to beef up their wealth-management capabilities and funds under management. The growth of superannuation funds also encouraged the banks to acquire funds managers. The big banks acquired smaller operations to tap into the Baby Boomers' super funds and create their own wealth-management businesses, with mixed results.

Meanwhile, smaller operations busied themselves merging or acquiring one another, often intending to become an attractive takeover target for the big banks. The best example was Colonial Mutual, which grew immensely in the 1990s under the leadership of Peter 'Pac-man' Smedley. (Smedley gained the nickname because of his voracious appetite for acquisitions.) Smedley's M&A spree led to Colonial Mutual appearing on the radar of the Commonwealth Bank, which paid around $9.4 billion for the former mutual society in 2000.

The Commonwealth Bank's acquisition of Colonial Mutual kicked off a buying spree, with NAB taking over MLC, ANZ linking with ING in a joint venture, and Westpac taking over BT Funds Management and Rothschild. There was also a host of smaller-scale takeovers. IOOF was a potential target but for the time-capped takeover clause in its demutualisation agreement.

While the banks were targeting superannuation and funds management businesses, rationalisation occurred among the smaller super funds managers. Corporate super funds consolidated as companies outsourced their funds to specialist providers due to rising costs and increased legislation.

Groups like the Guinness Peat Group–backed AWM were serial acquirers of smaller super funds, enabling them to scale quickly. AWM snowballed to become a significant force in superannuation funds management during the 2000s, especially after it merged with Select Managed Funds (SMF) in 2006. Before that, SMF, helmed by its managing director Christopher Kelaher, hoovered up a panoply of smaller funds, including United Funds Management, Pannell Kerr

Forster master funds, divisions of Citicorp's retail superannuation and non-super business, Mellon Human Resources & Investor Solutions master trust and many others. By 2007, AWM had $53.5 billion in funds under administration. Some journalists commented on the similarities between AWM's Kelaher and Colonial Mutual's Smedley.

Against this backdrop, IOOF was again looking for a CEO following Dewhurst's resignation, whose departure left IOOF looking vulnerable. Fund outflows from Perennial over the past year also contributed to the sense that IOOF needed to find a capable CEO quickly to retain market confidence. In early April 2007, IOOF unveiled Tony Robinson, who joined after a successful tenure as the managing director of the listed underwriter and insurance broker OAMPS. Before joining OAMPS, Robinson headed St George Bank's financial services platform operation Wealthpoint.

Talking to the *Australian Financial Review* about his appointment, Robinson was optimistic: 'The existing business is terrific. Ron has done a wonderful job.' He indicated he wanted to maintain an organic growth strategy rather than bulking up through acquisitions. 'Everyone loves organic growth because, in general, the return on

IOOF chief executive officer Tony Robinson was faced with tough decisions as the business responded to the GFC and deteriorating market conditions. Louise Kennerley/ *Australian Financial Review*

capital from organic growth will beat growth from acquisitions,' he told *Australian Financial Review*.[2]

Chair Ian Blair welcomed Robinson's appointment and pointed to his service-based industries expertise: 'In addition to financial services, Tony's experience in a broad array of service-based industries will also be a powerful complement to IOOF's "service first" approach to doing business with our clients.'[3]

Robinson brought a new perspective and set of skills to the mix. Dewhurst had been hired for his funds acumen and people management. Instead, Robinson brought a nuts-and-bolts approach to making the organisation tick, putting his mind towards integrating the gains made in funds management through Perennial with the burgeoning platforms and administration business.

Robinson reflected upon his arrival at IOOF in an interview for this book. Having been a director of Bendigo Bank, he was already familiar with IOOF and his predecessors, Turner and Dewhurst:

~

Rob Turner had a tremendous impact because he reduced the scope of the business. And I knew that Ron Dewhurst had really started to change the focus of the business towards funds management and had done so very successfully. He had deep expertise in that area. When I inherited the company, it had two parts of equal weighting, the funds management area and the platforms and administration.

~

Robinson said he was impressed by the talent at the organisation upon his arrival, with deep capability evident in the admin area, providing an opportunity for the business to be a significant player if it could get more scale. 'We had a good group of people in the business,' he said. 'The people doing the doing were exceptional, like Tony Hodges, Renato Mota and Peter Wallbridge, to name a few.'

In 2006, IOOF's share price was on a roller-coaster, reflecting the turbulence of international and domestic equity markets. The recent federal government incentives encouraging increased super contributions were smoothing out these ups and downs. The superannuation administration services business, IOOF Portfolio Solutions, saw an uplift in net inflows exceeding $250 million, an increase of more than 200 per cent over the previous year's results, offsetting falls on the Perennial side.

By 2007, several milestones across the group highlighted the substantial reshaping of the business. IOOF could point to another successful financial year, with funds under management and administration increasing by 14 per cent to $34.8 billion, and an underlying net profit (excluding the impact of Perennial and restructuring costs) after tax increasing by 26 per cent to $29.2 million. The full-year dividends increased by 22 per cent to 33 cents per share. The consolidated net profit for the 2006/07 year was $22.3 million, a little down on the previous year's result of $23.1 million.

The icing on the cake came with the Pursuit Select Personal Superannuation fund being awarded Best New Superannuation Product of the Year at the Rainmaker Marketing Excellence Awards and the Pursuit Select and Core Personal Superannuation funds receiving AAA ratings from Selecting Super.

Along with a new CEO, the board of directors underwent renewal. IOOF had appointed three new directors over the previous two years following the retirement of long-serving directors Michael Parkinson and Ray Schoer in 2005 and the departure of Dewhurst. The board now consisted of chair Ian Blair, deputy chair Roger Sexton, Mike Crivelli, Tony Hodges, Kate Spargo, Jane Harvey, James Pfeiffer, Rick Harper and Tony Robinson.

IOOF was in a sound position, but the economy and markets showed worrying instability. The strong equity-market performance of the previous few years was starting to weaken, with nervous signs emanating from overseas, especially the United States. In June 2007, IOOF undertook a $40-million capital raising to bolster the balance sheet and reduce debt resulting from the purchase of the minority shareholders of Perennial Partners.

By the end of the year, Australia had a new federal government, with Kevin Rudd leading the Labor Party to victory in the November 2007 election. There was some trepidation about the new government's economic direction. These concerns deepened as an economic crisis, soon dubbed the Global Financial Crisis (GFC), began to unfold.

Falling US house prices and a rising number of borrowers unable to repay their loans were the sparks that ignited the GFC. Financial system weaknesses first emerged around mid-2007, with American lenders and investors incurring significant losses because repossessed homes could only be sold at prices below the loan balance. These stress points in the US housing market soon spilled into mortgage-backed securities and, via the banking and financial sector, into more complex financial products such as collateralised debt obligations (CDOs) and credit default swaps. The ensuing credit crisis soon affected the US economy, and before long embroiled the world.

Robinson said the GFC was challenging for IOOF and similar funds management businesses in Australia:

~

Housing prices didn't collapse, but equity prices did. When equity prices collapse, your revenue collapses. Of course, at IOOF, in funds management and administration, you're charging a percentage of the assets under management or the funds under management. We were in a situation where everything changed with the GFC.

~

Robinson and the board had to think quickly about how IOOF could ride out the storm in the volatile funds management sector:

~

Did we want to increase the capital we put into that business? Did we have the expertise to do it other than by acquisition? Were we good at finding talented people to seed them into businesses, which Perennial had been doing? Did we have the distribution network to drive growth in those businesses? No, and that was a reminder of the volatility at play.

~

In February 2008, IOOF downgraded its full-year earnings outlook, reporting a 59 per cent tumble in net profit to $5.7 million for the six months to 31 December. 'While the IOOF businesses are performing strongly across all elements of the group, with good fund flows in the first half, our expectation is that the second-half revenue will be affected by lower funds under management and advice,' IOOF said in a media statement.

It was not only IOOF struggling, with the S&P/ASX 200 dropping 18 per cent since November 2007. Super fund inflows slowed to a trickle. IOOF suffered a $3.9-billion drop in funds under management and administration in the March quarter. The Australian share market recorded its biggest quarterly loss since the 1987 crash. Australian companies faced their tightest operating conditions in over a decade.

By May 2008, the rumour mill speculated that IOOF was a takeover target. One name consistently mentioned was AWM, which had grown into a similarly sized business to IOOF through an aggressive M&A regime over the past decade. AWM held a 2 per cent stake in IOOF, further fanning rumours.

Speaking to the *Australian Financial Review* in August, Robinson gave a subdued appraisal of inward-bound fund flows:

~

A lot of advisers get new clients from transitions, when people are retiring, when they are leaving a corporate or industry fund, and people are tending to stay in their jobs. So the number of new clients they are able to see is down and that means the funds flow to us is a little slower.[4]

~

IOOF started the new financial year with $29.4 billion in funds under management, well below the $34.8 billion in 2007. Funds under management and administration declined a further $1.9 billion to $27.5 billion in the September quarter. In the 2008 annual report, chair Ian Blair was stoic in his outlook:

~

Although our reported bottom line increased from the previous year, the real or underlying level of company profit fell to produce a disappointing profit result for our company . . . Whilst it is cold comfort to report this result, it is a fact that most of our competitor companies in the financial services sector experienced similar disappointing results.

~

The GFC was a slow burn in the first half of 2008. But in September 2008 the Lehman Brothers collapse and the failure of other firms sent global markets into meltdown. Investors pulled their money out of banks and investment funds worldwide, concerned about a Great Depression scenario.

The Rudd Government responded to the GFC in October 2008 with several economic stimulus packages to keep the Australian economy buoyant. Brendan Esposito/*The Sydney Morning Herald*

The board examined its options. Robinson recalled that the next step was to think seriously about a merger: 'The sensible thing to do was look for someone we could buy and get a step up in scale. And the logical one was Australian Wealth Management, which Chris Kelaher was running.'

On 24 November 2008, IOOF announced it was merging with AWM. Under the merger agreement, IOOF shareholders would own about 30 per cent of the merged entity, leaving AWM investors holding the majority 70 per cent stake. The merged group would have about $88 billion worth of assets under management. The combined group would keep the IOOF name, but Kelaher would lead, and his management team would come in. Kelaher told the media the combined entity 'would tick every box—demographic, regulatory and scale—and offer a fully vertically integrated financial services company'.[5]

In essence, the takeover was a reverse management acquisition. Robinson said maintaining management control was not an option, but the deal promised great returns to shareholders:

~

The economics of doing it, the benefit to shareholders of a deal, were going to be fantastic, like a 20 per cent increase in earnings per share out of the transaction before squeezing out any synergy benefits. So we approached them, offering to acquire them in a scrip-only deal, knowing that the challenge would be maintaining my role in the business.

~

Robinson was philosophical about the outcome, which saw him relinquish his role as CEO. He acknowledged that the nature of the deal was too compelling to pass up: 'We went into it knowing that Chris would end up with that role, but it gave us and the shareholders what we needed, which was this amazing step up and synergy benefits on top of it.'

The GFC may have nudged the merger along. Still, the M&A landscape of the Australian financial services industry had indicated it was only a matter of time before IOOF merged with someone. Once more, the organisation was on the cusp of a new era. Robinson said the decision to merge was the best for shareholders:

~

I always tell people that, as a managing director, you're wearing three hats. One is the hat of the shareholders. One is the hat of the business, the staff and the people. And the other is the hat of self-interest. It's very easy at moments like that to wear the wrong hat. It was evident at this moment self-interest wasn't the thing to focus on because the step-up in the benefits to the shareholders was so significant.

~

IOOF managing director Christopher Kelaher took over the role of chief executive in 2009 when IOOF merged with Australian Wealth Management. Kelaher was known for his dealmaking skills and led IOOF for a decade. *Australian Financial Review*

CHAPTER 16

THE DEALMAKER

C hristopher Kelaher began his tenure as IOOF managing director the same way he left off with AWM—doing deals. Even before starting on 30 April 2009, when he officially took over from Tony Robinson, he was working on a package deal for IOOF to buy platform administration firm Skandia and investment management business Intech from Old Mutual Group for about $34 million. AWM provided IOOF with a $10-million loan for the deal.

With the AWM merger and the acquisitions of Skandia and Intech, IOOF had $94.6 billion in funds under management, administration, advice and supervision by the end of the 2008/09 financial year—an incredible leap from the previous year's $34.8 billion. Skandia soon rebranded as IOOF Global One, and Intech was sold to Morningstar Australasia Limited. The funds under management and administration increase put IOOF into a different league. Either directly or indirectly, the company was now servicing around 700,000 Australians.

The leap in scale came at a fortuitous time as small and medium-sized financial services companies emerged from the GFC counting their losses and nervous about the future. The GFC lingered, but signs of recovery in global equity markets were apparent. By the start of 2009, governments were pumping liquidity into the financial system to keep credit flowing and revive consumer confidence. Australian finance businesses generally were in a better position than their US counterparts: the China-fuelled minerals boom and the Rudd government's fiscal stimulus strategy had buffered the economy.

The IOOF and AWM merger was a good match: IOOF brought legacy, expertise and industry goodwill to the table; AWM brought funds, scale and Kelaher, who had a reputation as a tenacious dealmaker. However, the merger involved significant turnover at the board and executive levels and some cultural tensions.

At the board level, non-executive directors Kate Spargo and Rick Harper departed, and Tony Hodges stepped down to an executive position. AWM directors replaced these retiring directors. The board now consisted of chair Ian Blair, deputy chair Roger Sexton, executive director Christopher Kelaher, James Pfeiffer, George Venardos, Jane Harvey and Ian Griffiths.

The management changes were even more sweeping. The headline grabber was Kelaher replacing Robinson as CEO, but the departures included chief financial officer Mark Blackburn; general counsel Adrianna Bisogni; company secretary Bill Linehan; head of compliance Malcolm Coe; head of risk Gavin Wood; and general manager of human resources Peter Wallbridge.

Interviewed for this book, Bisogni said the employees understood that the merger involved a management takeover: 'The agreement was that Chris would be coming in with his team. I was under no illusions. Everybody knew that the IOOF executive team, for the most part, would not be around post acquisition.'

The restructure involved IOOF dismantling its four-person, Sydney-based investment team and creating a newly staffed group based in Melbourne. In September, Telstra Super's chief investment officer, Steve Merlicek, joined as chief investment officer. Merlicek took over from Hodges, who finished his stellar career with IOOF at the end of 2009.

Hodges' 33-year securities industry career spanned merchant banking and investment management. He'd held senior positions with Chase AMP, AMP Morgan Grenfell Acceptances and AMP Discount Corporation before joining the IOOF Group in 1985 as head of investments. In September 2004, he was appointed executive director of several group subsidiaries. He was also one of the founding directors of Perennial Investment Partners. Previous chairs and chief executives consistently turned to him for advice. For many, Hodges was the heart and soul of IOOF.

The GFC dragged on for a few years but by 2010 the economy was turning around, businesses were optimistic, and consumers began spending again.
Dan Peled/AAP Image

He had arrived at IOOF when Martyn Pickersgill started modernising the friendly society. Former CEO Robert Turner described Hodges as a 'star of the funds management industry. He was leading the way for IOOF to get involved in that business. Tony was a guru in the industry, and I leaned on his knowledge and wisdom.'

Long-term board member Roger Sexton worked closely with Hodges for over a decade. 'Tony was instrumental in driving the organisation from being a sleepy financial services organisation to a listed public company,' Sexton said in an interview for this book. Hodges was also a mentor to many, with a future IOOF CEO counting him as one of his formative influences.

The shareholder composition was also changing. Bruce Neill, who founded Select Managed Funds, emerged with a 12.1 per cent stake in IOOF Holdings. Neill had a 39 per cent holding in Select, which AWM had taken over in June 2006. Kelaher had been CEO of Select and continued in that position following the Select and AWM merger. Bendigo and Adelaide Bank also maintained substantial holdings.

The merger complicated reporting on 2008/09 financials, but the results showed promise. The reported underlying net profit after tax of $23.1 million was not a true reflection of the earnings base of the new group. Had the merger happened at the beginning of the financial year, the result would have been nearer $52 million. The chair's report struck a positive note:

~

Despite the global downturn, I remain firmly of the opinion that the wealth management industry will continue to survive and prosper. Ensuring your financial future well beyond retirement is still as important as ever, and I believe IOOF will be there for its clients for many years to come. Against the backdrop of the worst financial crisis seen in recent times, IOOF is taking advantage of the downturn to rejuvenate its business, ensuring it is well positioned for the market recovery and beyond.

~

By the end of 2009, the new IOOF was finding its feet. Despite continuing issues with net funds outflows, its shares increased more than 50 per cent over the year, buoyed by improving equity markets. However, the rumour mill continued to churn, with talk of ANZ scoping IOOF as an acquisition target. Yet the *Australian Financial Review* referred to the newly merged IOOF in less than flattering terms:

~

ANZ has run the slide rule over IOOF before and the funds manager failed to snag any concrete interest then, largely because its motley crew of assets (described by some as 14 or so platforms held together with a piece of sticky tape and a Band-Aid) was seen as run-down and unlikely to provide enough scale to make a difference. The fact is IOOF isn't just one entity but a group of entities formed after Select Managed Funds merged with Australian Wealth Management (previously part of Tower Australia), which then merged with IOOF (and then they bought Skandia). IOOF chief executive Chris Kelaher, the former boss of SMF, is seen in the industry as something of a merger junkie. For a Big Four bank, that's a lot of fiddly bolt-ons to integrate down the track.[1]

~

This commentary reflected some industry thoughts about IOOF's potential to unite into a cohesive whole. Scepticism remained that this new IOOF could emerge as a serious standalone competitor. Could Kelaher and his new management team successfully consolidate platforms, streamline administration and combine the IOOF and AWM teams to produce more than the sum of its parts? Was it held together by more than 'sticky tape and a Band-Aid'? Would IOOF become a major player or collapse beneath the weight of its conceit, a financial Frankenstein's monster?

Meanwhile, the financial services industry was undergoing its periodic bout of political scrutiny and regulatory reforms. Three significant reviews were taking place: the Future of Financial Advice (FOFA) review, the Henry Review into taxation and the Cooper Review into superannuation. On top of platform consolidations, cost reductions and the cultural challenges of a merged organisation, Kelaher had to negotiate the upcoming round of regulatory changes from the reviews.

In August 2010, the company agreed on terms to acquire the North investment platform business from AXA Asia Pacific. The acquisition was contingent on the ACCC approving the $13.3-billion merger between NAB and AXA Asia Pacific.

One industry super fund executive criticised IOOF in an anonymous submission to the ACCC merger review. As reported by the *Australian Financial Review*, the executive said: 'It will be some years before it becomes clear if IOOF can be successful at its current scale. It would be even longer before it becomes clear if it can acquire another business, such as the North platform, and be successful.' An IOOF spokesperson responded: 'It is clear that whoever has written this submission suffers from a combination of selective perception disorder and convenient short-term memory loss.'[2]

Furthermore, the *Australian Financial Review* reported:

~

One of the submissions from a top industry fund claims the abolition of commissions would require IOOF to undertake a 'major re-engineering' of its business at a time when it should focus on integrating the North platform. The fund declined to be named. An IOOF spokesman said: 'This claim underscores whoever wrote the submission doesn't understand the business. Conversion to fee-for-service commission is straightforward and IOOF has achieved this with two of its flagship products.'[3]

~

In the end, the ACCC rejected the NAB and AXA Asia Pacific merger, meaning IOOF could not acquire the North platform. It was a knockback for the business, but Kelaher considered the deal opportunistic rather than strategically integral. The submissions to the ACCC underlined a growing enmity towards IOOF among some quarters of the superannuation industry.

IOOF was developing into a sizeable competitor within the superannuation industry. Kelaher was an ambitious CEO, not content with fiddling around the edges or settling for second-best. His forthright approach was on display again in February 2011, when he told the *Australian Financial Review* that the federal government was 'dumbing down' superannuation with reforms such as the low-cost MySuper option, a recommendation of the Cooper Review.

A couple of months later, Kelaher was again outspoken about the government's proposed 'future of financial advice' reforms to end conflicts on remuneration, introduce a 'best interest' test, strengthen investor rights and boost regulators' powers. He said the proposed reforms would lead to unintended consequences that would disadvantage unaligned financial advisers rather than help them. 'This has not been well thought through and the bad logic has been getting worse,' he said.[4]

In June 2011, Kelaher once more took a bat to the government's reform agenda. He told the *Australian Financial Review* that the government was attempting to micromanage the industry, and that the FOFA reforms had 'nothing to do with consumers' and only served to give industry funds a leg up into financial advice:

~

Look back at the global financial crisis and the success of the local banks, which was unprecedented anywhere in the world,' Mr Kelaher said. 'The scary thing is a minority government now wants to fix things. If you parachuted in from another planet, you would be very scared.' Mr Kelaher has called on the six independents sitting on the House of Representatives cross-benches to oppose the legislation that is expected to be tabled later this year. 'It gets dangerous if you permit government to micromanage business and industry,' Mr Kelaher said. 'I'm advocating that they should reject FOFA 100 per cent because there's too much micro-management. It does not have merit . . . Do we need legislation? No we don't,' he said. 'The industry has already responded.[5]

~

Between his critiques of government policy, Kelaher continued to acquire and consolidate. In the latter half of 2011, IOOF completed a $94-million takeover of DKN Financial, in which IOOF already had a substantial shareholding, and Kelaher was a director. The acquisition boosted adviser numbers to over a thousand and gave a bump to funds under advice.

Some in the markets now viewed Kelaher's disciplined approach, prudent cost-cutting and eye for value acquisitions as a winning combination. 'We continue to see IOOF as a well-run, high cash-generating business with exposure to growth from equity market

The mining boom helped to keep the Australian economy in reasonable shape despite the global downturn. Taras Vyshnya/Alamy

returns and legislated superannuation contributions,' one Deutsche Bank analyst said.[6]

The 2011 annual report delivered robust numbers, showing the business was on track and that the worst of the GFC was over. The company's market capitalisation was at $1.5 billion. It had 984 employees. Funds under management, advice and supervision totalled $106.2 billion, and the number of clients was around 700,000. IOOF reported a net profit after tax of $99.5 million and an underlying net profit after tax and pre-amortisation result of $111.5 million. The revenue split was 60 per cent from platform management and administration, 30 per cent from investment management, 6 per cent from financial advice and distribution and 4 per cent from trustee and estate services. James Pfeiffer retired from the board after six years of service. Kevin White, the former CEO of WHK Group, filled Pfeiffer's seat.

Significant board and executive level changes marked the first two years of the merged group. Consolidating platforms, products and services occupied a substantial portion of time and effort as Kelaher and his team pruned overlaps and sheared unprofitable units.

The group's property footprint was reduced, bringing more employees into the 161 Collins Street head office. Despite the tepid post-GFC conditions, the company kept shareholders happy. Between June 2009 and June 2011, the total shareholder return (a combination of total dividends paid and share price movement over the period) was 76 per cent, or 33 per cent annualised.

At the AGM on 23 November 2011, IOOF chair Ian Blair announced his resignation:

~

It is with mixed feelings that I have decided not to stand for re-election next year. Instead, I will retire from my duties as Chairman and a non-executive Director of IOOF in 2012. At that time, Dr Roger Sexton, a current Non-Executive Director and Deputy Chairman, will assume the Chairmanship. I am personally very proud of IOOF's growth throughout my tenure on the Board, first as a non-executive Director and later as Chairman. During my time on the Board, I have seen Net Profit After Tax increase from $8 million prior to listing to $99m last financial year.

~

Blair had been a non-executive director of IOOF since 2000 and was previously a director of IOOF Trustees Ltd. He served on several board committees and was a director of Perennial Investment Partners Ltd. He had provided level-headed guidance as chair since 2005, helping consolidate IOOF as a listed entity and through various acquisitions and mergers, including AWM.

Blair's departure was another loosening of ties with the pre-AWM merger IOOF. Sexton and Jane Harvey were now the only board members in place from before the AWM merger. Sexton was the only one connected to IOOF's friendly society days.

IOOF chairman Dr Roger Sexton was first involved with the business in the mid-1990s when he advised on the takeover of the OST Friendly Society. He resigned as IOOF chair in November 2016. Penny Stephens/*The Sydney Morning Herald*

CHAPTER 17

REGULATORY REFORMS AND MEDIA TRIBULATIONS

D r Roger Sexton's history with IOOF started in the troubled mid-1990s, when the friendly society struggled to integrate the OST Friendly Society. Sexton earned a reputation as a Mr Fixit for his work as the Asset Management Task Force chair, overseeing the sale of over $5 billion in public-sector assets in South Australia.

In the 1990s, IOOF needed Sexton's help selling non-performing OST assets and restructuring the balance sheet. After he finished his consultancy work, the board invited him to become a non-executive director in 1996. He was also the chair of IOOF Trustees for several years and a director of Perennial Investment Partners.

Sexton worked alongside David Jury, Lindsay Bytheway, Robert Turner, Tony Hodges, Ray Schoer and others to guide the organisation from being a conservative, Victorian-based friendly society to a publicly listed national financial services business. He was involved in many decisions that led IOOF to demutualisation and listing. He became deputy chair in 2002 and chair after Ian Blair's resignation in 2012.

At the start of 2012, IOOF brought a portion of its $9-billion multi-manager portfolio in-house. Another focus of the new investment strategy was to push into the self-managed superannuation fund (SMSF) sector. Rivals were finding it hard to turn a dollar from the SMSF sector. However, Kelaher believed IOOF could become a significant player in this fractured sector. While embarking on these forays, IOOF reduced its investment platforms from eight to three and consolidated its technology systems.

By the end of the 2011/12 financial year, IOOF had a market cap of $1.4 billion, 1040 employees, $107.3 billion in funds under management and supervision, and more than 600,000 clients serviced through its platforms, products and services. Its affiliated financial advisers numbered 990, provided chiefly through Bridges Financial Services, Wealth Managers, Ord Minnett Stockbrokers and Consultum Financial Advisers. In 2012, Lonsdale Financial Group joined this division courtesy of IOOF's acquisition of DKN.

In the 2012 annual report, the new chair expressed optimism about the organisation's resilience in handling regulatory changes and capacity for growth:

Pleasingly, the IOOF group has continued to perform solidly through the period—in part because our products, systems, people and culture have been attuned over a long period of time to adapt to changes in the financial and regulatory environment in which we operate . . . The corporate history of IOOF shows that while we have been quite aggressive in taking advantage of deep value acquisition opportunities as and when they become available from time to time, the business itself has always been very conservatively managed.

~

In June 2012, FOFA reforms were introduced into the *Corporations Act* (2001) by the *Corporations Amendment (Future of Financial Advice) Act* (2012) and the *Corporations Amendment (Further Future of Financial Advice Measures) Act* (2012). These reforms included the best interests duty, ban on conflicted forms of remuneration, opt-in obligation and changes to ASIC's licensing and banning powers. The reforms imposed significant further costs on the financial services sector.

Clive Palmer MP struck a deal with the federal government to keep new rules on financial advice as part of the Future of Financial Advice reforms introduced by the former Labor government. Lukas Coch/AAP Image

Kelaher mentioned the impost of the regulatory reforms on the business in the 2012 annual report:

~

The large volume of regulatory reform remains a challenge for the entire financial services industry . . . many key elements of these reforms have not been announced or finalised by the regulators, making implementation by the set deadlines particularly difficult. IOOF is well placed to respond to these regulatory changes as a business.

~

Regulatory reform was an additional hurdle to expediting things for a business seeking to grow as quickly as IOOF. Kelaher's strategy was to consistently maintain a lean organisational structure that could pounce upon opportunities as they presented. Acquisitions involved intense periods of integration and consolidation, and working through extensive regulatory requirements. To continue doing this successfully, Kelaher and his team required certainty from regulators.

IOOF had acquired the financial advisory group DKN in September 2011, and then the wealth-management firm Plan B in July 2012. IOOF paid $96 million for DKN and $49.1 million for Plan B. Avenue Capital Advisers, a smaller firm, was also absorbed into the business. The acquisitions boosted aligned adviser numbers and increased funds under management and administration. They significantly provided access to two of Australia's high-growth states, Western Australia and Queensland, and brought a more substantial presence in New Zealand.

Improving workplace diversity was another key focus in 2012. Understanding that the financial services industry had long been male-dominated, IOOF sought to start redressing the gender imbalance within the organisation and committed to championing workplace diversity. A policy was put in place to increase the representation of women in senior roles and provide more opportunities for Indigenous Australians, people from culturally and linguistically diverse backgrounds, people from lower socioeconomic backgrounds and people with a disability.

Danielle Corcoran, the Head of Human Resources and Company Secretary, worked with a gender equality committee to drive initiatives to foster and develop women into senior roles. IOOF had one woman on the board then, and only two in senior executive positions. A pay equity audit was also conducted among all levels of staff to determine how IOOF could remedy the gender pay gap. After becoming chair of the board, Sexton made it a priority to correct the gender gap. In 2015, IOOF signed up to the Australian Institute of Company Directors (AICD) 30 Percent Club, which aimed to increase the number of women on boards in Australia by setting a target of 30 per cent for all S&P/ASX 200 boards by 2018.

On 30 January 2013, Prime Minister Julia Gillard announced that a federal election would be held in September; the unusually long lead time created uncertainty in the financial services industry. Could plans be made for policies and regulations the Gillard government wanted to implement? Or would the election campaign be a dead period dominated by soundbites and vague promises? The leadership tensions within the Labor Party did not help matters. Subsequently, Kevin Rudd succeeded Julia Gillard as prime minister on 27 June. On 7 September, the Coalition defeated the Labor government in a landslide win, installing a new prime minister, Tony Abbott.

The election result provided clarity for the financial services industry. Chair Roger Sexton noted in the 2013 annual report:

~

Governments cannot expect retirees to take responsibility for their own retirement incomes, rather than be a burden on the public purse, via the pension, if they keep changing the rules . . . I welcome the fact that the recently elected Coalition Government has committed to delivering more certainty around superannuation policy, effectively promising no 'negative, unexpected changes'. This commitment is essential to promote stability in the superannuation system and gives Australians the confidence to invest in superannuation without fear of constant change.

~

By 2013, IOOF's market cap was $1.7 billion. Employee numbers increased to 1300, and funds under management and supervision hit $120.2 billion. The Plan B and DKN acquisitions were bedded in, resulting in a 14 per cent uplift in the dividend rate to 42 cents per share. IOOF's expertise in integrating acquisitions meant the transition occurred seamlessly and efficiently. Outside the Big Four

In January 2013, Prime Minister Julia Gillard announced that a federal election would be held in September. The long campaign time created uncertainty for financial markets. Kym Smith/Newspix

banks, IOOF was now among a handful of Australia's largest and most successful independent financial services organisations.

The year's results also saw the first positive net fund flow since the transformative Skandia and AWM acquisitions in 2009, an important milestone for the group that represented a significant advance in organic growth from previous years. The slow recovery of the international and domestic economies meant equity prices boosted investment returns and funds under management. The signposted gradual increase in Australia's compulsory superannuation to 12 per cent (by 2025) underpinned continued growth in the asset pool, benefiting the funds manager and platform businesses like IOOF. By the end of 2013, IOOF's market cap hit $2.1 billion. It was now hovering around the top 100 ASX companies.

The change in the company, especially in its size, ambition and focus, was noted by Maria Bonham-Gilberd, who previously worked at IOOF between 2005 and 2008. Bonham-Gilberd worked under Ron Dewhurst and briefly Tony Robinson before moving to ANZ for a few years. She returned to IOOF in 2013.

Interviewed for this book, she said the business appeared to have moved up a gear under Kelaher. She recalled that the company was successfully meeting a raft of regulatory and governance targets on her return:

~

As per my previous experience at IOOF, everyone was still extraordinarily busy. There were many regulatory delivery projects, as there always are, but especially in that period. People had been brought in to lead quite significant pieces of change in that regard, the work was large and complex, but the teams continued to deliver. IOOF had at its heart, a real drive to succeed into the next phase of its growth.

~

She also noted that the organisation had shaken off some of the old friendly society attitudes, and employees were displaying more confidence about IOOF's place in the financial services industry. She said: 'There was a change. It felt like it had matured and started to become a significant player. The people around the organisation seemed more seasoned and were very focused.'

Kelaher might have appeared less collegial than some of his predecessors, but he seemed to have trust in his senior team and gave them leeway in decision-making. Pathways also seemed to be there for some of the more junior managers to succeed. Bonham-Gilberd recalled: 'Those around Chris were flourishing. I'm not sure whether that's just because they were flourishing because, individually, they would've done anyway. But many people were taking on much bigger roles, doing bigger things and being afforded opportunities.'

The 2014 annual report recorded that IOOF was now an ASX 100 company with a market cap of $1.9 billion. The $670-million acquisition of financial advice and wealth-management firm SFG Australia (SFGA) in May 2014 allowed IOOF entry into the high-net-worth client sector. SFGA's $13.8 billion in funds under advice significantly improved organic funds flow. Some of the year's key highlights included a $123-million underlying net profit after tax and pre-amortisation result—a 13 per cent increase on the previous year and a $1.4-billion net funds inflow into platforms. IOOF's operating segments—namely, financial advice, platform, investment management and trustee services—experienced an increase in revenue and profitability from the last financial year. IOOF's cost-to-income ratio fell by 1.2 per cent to 57.5 per cent.

The six-person board remained stable during the years when Sexton was chair. In 2014, Allan Griffiths joined the board, taking over from Kevin White. After serving three years as an independent director, White resigned to focus on his other corporate interests and responsibilities. Griffiths joined IOOF with over 30 years of experience in the financial services industry and a deep understanding of the insurance sector. He had held several executive positions within the industry, most notably as long-term CEO of Aviva Australia and later Managing Director, South East Asia, Aviva Pty Ltd. Before joining Aviva, he held executive positions with Norwich Union and Colonial Limited.

After years of tinkering with the superannuation system, IOOF was hopeful the federal government would tread lightly with any further regulation. In November 2014, the Financial System Inquiry, chaired by former Commonwealth Bank chief David Murray, delivered its final report. The report made recommendations on all elements of the financial system, but of especial pertinence to IOOF were those relating to financial advice and superannuation. Kelaher expressed his views to the media, saying the review 'really got it wrong when it painted Australia's superannuation system as one of the most expensive in the world', and that it 'had a misguided focus on fees rather than outcomes'.[1]

In the middle of 2015, IOOF underwent a period of intense media scrutiny sparked by unfounded allegations. On 20 June 2015, Fairfax journalists Adele Ferguson and Sarah Danckert laid out a series of claims against IOOF in *The Sydney Morning Herald* and the *Australian Financial Review*.[2] They based their allegations on documents stolen from IOOF by an apparent whistleblower. IOOF, particularly the Bridges Financial Advice research team, was accused of insider trading, front-running, plagiarism, cross-selling shares at inflated prices and trading across Chinese Walls. The accusations extended to IOOF failing to report these breaches to ASIC and failing to support the whistleblower who had alerted them to these issues.

Labor senator Sam Dastyari and Nationals senator John Williams jumped on the stories, making statements in the Senate under parliamentary privilege on 24 June 2015 about the 'appalling behaviour of IOOF'. The company received a summons for its leaders to appear before the Senate Committee of Inquiry into Financial Services. On 3 July 2015, Kelaher appeared before the committee, as Sexton was overseas. He cooperated and answered all relevant questions, but the perception among some was that he was aloof and combative.

Sexton appeared before the Senate Committee on 3 August 2015. That morning, the chair of the committee, Senator Dastyari, went on ABC Radio and said, 'What you have is a culture of cover-up within IOOF which frankly appears to go to the top.'[3] Dastyari's inflammatory remarks set the scene for the Senate hearing that morning.

Interviewed for this book, Sexton said:

~

When the questioning moved on to the issue of how IOOF had treated whistleblowers, I made it known that I had been a whistleblower three times in my corporate career. I made the point to the committee that I know how whistleblowers should behave. In this case, the supposed whistleblower did not follow the standards of behaviour expected of a whistleblower. The fact that I had been a whistleblower myself, in well-documented circumstances, took the committee by surprise and, without a doubt, took the wind out of their criticisms.

~

Kelaher and Sexton provided testimony that made clear, firstly, that IOOF's compliance processes had previously identified the majority of the issues raised and thoroughly investigated them. Secondly, no IOOF client lost money through any actions IOOF staff took during the fifteen years in question. As events subsequently transpired, the accusations were shown to be unfounded and part of an opportunistic media blow-up instigated by a disaffected employee.

In July 2016, ASIC finalised its inquiries into the allegations, including those raised by a former employee. In its formal statement, ASIC announced it would take no further action but said the review had:

~

. . . identified a number of concerns relating to IOOF's compliance arrangements, breach reporting, management of conflicts of interest, staff trading policy, disclosure, whistleblower management and protection and cyber security. We have raised these concerns with IOOF. We have also advised IOOF that in our view the corporate culture at that time within IOOF contributed to these issues occurring.[4]

~

IOOF always maintained it had thoroughly investigated these concerns and, where appropriate, taken decisive action. The episode took a toll on those involved and on the morale of IOOF employees, who were tired of seeing the company dragged through the media mud.

Sexton recalled the intense scrutiny and felt that Fairfax Media had maltreated IOOF:

~

The majority of the alleged compliance breaches reported in the media between 1998 and 2009 occurred in a company [AWM] that IOOF did not own at the time. All of the alleged breaches were matters that were known about by IOOF. Indeed they were discovered by internal compliance processes and procedures and thoroughly investigated. None was found to be illegal. Some were found to be in breach of policies and procedures that existed in the company at the time, and where this was the case, appropriate action was taken.

Notwithstanding the insinuations of the press, not one single client of IOOF had lost money through any actions taken by staff at IOOF. Mistakes can and will be made. Oversights do occur, and rules can be broken. That is why we have formal investigative and compliance structures in place. We all knew we were speaking the truth when we said IOOF had done nothing wrong. It just took a long and emotionally draining process for us to prove this to everyone else and counteract the misplaced sensationalism.

~

The public attention reinforced the need for the company to remain vigilant in its compliance responsibilities and enhance its governance procedures. For this reason, IOOF appointed PricewaterhouseCoopers (PwC) to review its internal compliance processes, with all the subsequent recommendations implemented unconditionally. Following the episode, IOOF welcomed the opportunity to interact with the industry regulators, ASIC and APRA, at an even more elevated level than usual to ensure a strong culture of compliance based on transparency and openness.

Sexton, Kelaher and other board members and executives endeavoured to set the record straight with stakeholders, including regulators at APRA and ASIC. Feeling like IOOF was not getting a fair hearing in the media, Sexton set up a series of private meetings to discuss the allegations and related issues with regulators and other relevant stakeholders across the spectrum of politics, business and the finance industry.

With the ASIC inquiry finalised, everyone wanted to return to business as usual. Speaking to *Investor Daily*, Kelaher said the company had implemented PwC's recommendations and was ready to move on: 'Basically it was a fairly straightforward exercise upon review. That's very much behind us, and ASIC provided a bookend with their commentary of no action.'[5]

Sexton resigned as chair in November 2016 after serving fifteen highly successful years as a director. He had contributed significantly to IOOF and helped guide the organisation from its days as a friendly society to becoming one of Australia's largest and most successful financial services businesses. 'I worked with many wonderful people at IOOF and I retain a great affection for many of them and the organisation today,' he said.

The Royal Commission into Misconduct in the Banking, Superannuation and Financial Services Industry, established on 14 December 2017, tested IOOF and the financial services industry. IOOF was one of the companies under the spotlight during the fifth round, which focused on superannuation. David Geraghty/AAP Image

CHAPTER 18

KELAHER'S LAST STAND

I n 2016, IOOF celebrated 170 years of helping Australians achieve financial independence. It now operated in a very different environment to 1846. It was Australia's largest independent financial services group, an ASX top-100 company with $131.1 billion in funds under management and administration.

However, the essence of its mission remained. The 2016 annual report proudly stated:

~

Since our beginnings in the 19th century—when we visited the sick, relieved the distressed, helped bury loved ones and educated orphans— our goal has always been to put clients first. We do this by seeking to understand their needs, look after them and provide solutions to help them secure their financial future.

~

A link to the friendly society days was maintained with the IOOF Foundation, which continued assisting disadvantaged communities. In 2016, the foundation surpassed the $12.5-million mark in total donations to charities since its formal establishment in 2001, following IOOF's demutualisation. Rob Turner and Lindsay Bytheway were instrumental in its creation. IOOF established the foundation as a philanthropic arm that would continue the charity work that characterised the organisation when it was a friendly society. The foundation also allowed IOOF staff to give back through community service initiatives.

IOOF now comprised four distinct business areas: financial advice and distribution services; platform management and administration; investment management; and trustee services. The financial advice branch of the business consisted of Bridges, Consultum, IOOF Alliances, Lonsdale, Ord Minnett and Shadforth. The platform management and administration branch consisted of IOOF Employer Super, IOOF Platform Connect and IOOF Pursuit. The investment-management branch consisted of IOOF MultiMix, IOOF QuantPlus and IOOF WealthBuilder. Australian Executor Trustees handled the trustee services.

The previous five years saw substantial changes to the business mix, with a concerted effort to consolidate acquired businesses and rationalise platforms. As a result, administration costs were contained without hampering the capacity for organic growth.

A three-pillared strategy of efficiency, organic growth and growth through acquisition proved resilient and delivered consistently solid results for shareholders. Statutory profit for the 2015/16 financial year was $196.8 million, up 42 per cent, translating into a record total dividend for the full year of 54.5 cents per share. The company's continued success was anchored in its capacity to swiftly integrate acquisitions into the broader group. Improved economic conditions also helped.

The wealth-management sector was experiencing challenging market conditions, but the sector's fundamentals were positive. A bipartisan political agreement on superannuation underpinned growth. By this time, Australians were starting to understand better the importance of super and the value of financial advice. Through education and the reality of a looming retirement for Baby Boomers, more Australians were taking an interest in their super funds than ever before. By mid-2016, the total value of accumulated superannuation savings in Australia was around $2.1 trillion.

In response, IOOF stepped up its commitment to ongoing professional development for all staff involved in this vital activity.

Members of the Shadforth financial advice team, part of the IOOF Group, take part in a community bike ride event. Insignia Financial

The IOOF Advice Academy was launched in July 2016 as a training and coaching resource for financial planning businesses and advisers. The initiative was driven by Renato Mota, IOOF's Group General Manager, Wealth Management, and Dean Lombardo, an award-winning financial planner. Its launch was another example of IOOF's commitment to providing the best advice to Australians seeking to secure their financial future.

The Perennial divestments undertaken the previous year reshaped the investment-management business, significantly reducing exposure to volatile institutional fund flows. The sale of two Perennial boutique businesses to the Henderson Group for $71.6 million (plus further payments tied to future performance) significantly contributed to the year's strong results. The sales realised a post-tax profit on the sale of $56 million. Many smaller transactions realised an additional $8 million, which enabled a further focus on core wealth-management capabilities. It was the end of an era as Perennial's importance to the group had gradually declined. Once IOOF's prime engine of growth, Perennial was sidelined as other funds managers were used and the platform and administration sides of the business grew.

Total net funds inflow was $1.8 billion to 30 June 2016. IOOF had now chalked up fourteen consecutive quarters of positive platform net inflows. Cost control remained a signature element of performance, reflected in a 56.9 per cent cost-to-income ratio. The strong balance sheet allowed IOOF to capitalise on future acquisition opportunities.

IOOF's open architecture platforms enabled it to offer non-IOOF products and services alongside its own, serving the best interests of clients and advisers. It was a fundamental differentiator in the advice sector.

The ClientFirst initiative was also part of the strategic push to engage with advisers and clients. In developing ClientFirst, IOOF listened to over 2000 client calls and reviewed over 3000 transactions to understand clients' needs fully. The data gathered enabled IOOF to provide valuable feedback to advisers on how to serve their clients best.

Another significant milestone was achieved in 2016 with the consolidation of the TPS platform into IOOF Pursuit, one of Australia's largest-ever platform transformations, with $7.1 billion of client funds transferred across 40,000 accounts. The project underlined the ability of the organisation to undertake large-scale transformational activities. With platform consolidation completed towards the end of the year and the highly positive flows experienced during the year, IOOF was poised for a strong 2017.

After seeing IOOF through intense media scrutiny, Roger Sexton retired from the board at the AGM on 24 November 2016. George Venardos took over as chair. An experienced company director in the financial services industry, he knew the business well. For ten years he was the chief financial officer of Insurance Australia Group and chair of the Insurance Council of Australia's Finance and Accounting Committee.

In a strange twist, Venardos was appointed chair of the tourism and leisure company Ardent Group in September 2016. As the Ardent chair, he was tasked with restoring the company's reputation after a tragic incident at Dreamworld theme park. Of course, Dreamworld was among the suite of assets IOOF inherited from OST in 1990 and sold in 1996. Having provided a steady hand at Ardent during a testing period, he retired from the chair's role in late 2017 to focus on IOOF.

Venardos joined the IOOF board at the time of the merger with AWM. Earlier in his career, he was NRMA's chief financial officer when it was demutualised and listed in 2000. He recalled when interviewed for this book that IOOF still carried elements of its friendly society days when he arrived:

In his role as chair, George Venardos had the difficult job of leading IOOF during the Royal Commission. Insignia Financial

I saw a lot of parallels in the culture of IOOF and NRMA. The great aspects of it were that it was customer driven. The customer came first, second and third, and the ethos of contributing to the community was strong, too. And there are still attributes of that in the IOOF and NRMA cultures.

According to Venardos, the downside of the friendly society legacy included higher costs:

It had far greater resources than it needed. It was bloated and a very comfortable environment for everyone who worked there. But quite frankly, the expense ratio was very high. And as a result, they struggled to find the capital to invest in systems, which was fundamental to the future.

He said the AWM and IOOF merger had worked well, with the IOOF brand carrying the merged group forward. 'That was the transaction and the proposition put to the IOOF board,' he recalled. 'They got the chairman; we [AWM] got the CEO and COO. They got three board positions and the succession of the chair role. And we got the CEO, CFO and one non-exec, which was me.'

Venardos said the merger combined two strong talent pools, including Kelaher's skills as a dealmaker: 'Chris Kelaher must have done something like a hundred acquisitions in his tenure in the nineteen years he was with the groups. That continual increase in scale was very beneficial for superannuation members, policyholders and shareholders.' However, he said Kelaher's approach to cost control was initially not well received by some at IOOF:

It took a long time for that board to settle down because it's not easy to hear that you're bloated, spending too much, and not in the right areas. But that was the very strong message that Kelaher was giving the board. And he was struggling to get the support of the joint board to unanimously pursue expense reduction to generate the capital to invest. He took quite a few percentage points out of the expense ratio and invested heavily in the bespoke proprietary computerised administration system they still use today.

~

Kelaher convinced the board of his vision, and the organisation's ongoing success vindicated him. IOOF built on its solid financials and positive business momentum. Outstanding funds growth, exceptional cost control and reliable underlying business performance metrics ensured an upward trajectory. Its advice-led strategy, multi-brand model and unique open architecture made it an attractive alternative for advisers looking to partner with a non-bank-aligned dealer group.

The underlying profit for the 2016/17 financial year was $169.4 million, translating into a total dividend for the full year of 53 cents per share, fully franked, for shareholders. In 2017, IOOF recorded an eighteenth consecutive quarter of positive platform net inflows, with $1.2 billion, an increase of 130 per cent compared to 2016. Adviser numbers grew, counter to industry trends. Advice net inflows of $3 billion, up 131 per cent compared to 2016, included $976 million from 33 new advisers joining IOOF from another licensee. Furthermore, in 2017, fourteen of the top 50 advisers in Barron's Top 50 Adviser awards were employed by or aligned with IOOF, underlining that IOOF-aligned advisers delivered high-quality financial advice and superior client outcomes.

The business continued simplifying and streamlining, divesting several smaller non-core businesses in 2017. In June 2017, IOOF acquired National Australia Trustees Ltd. The acquisition demonstrated IOOF's commitment to building its trustee business and made IOOF Australia's largest compensation trusts provider.

The board experienced turnover at this time, with two new non-executive directors joining over the past two years. The board now consisted of chair George Venardos, managing director Christopher Kelaher, and non-executive directors Elizabeth Flynn, Jane Harvey, Allan Griffiths and John Selak.

Flynn joined in 2015, bringing over 30 years of experience in the financial services industry, including roles in law, corporate governance, and executive responsibilities. From 1998 to 2010, she was the Chief Legal Counsel, Group Compliance Manager and Group

Company Secretary of Aviva Australia and a director of NULIS Nominees, Aviva Australia's superannuation trustee company.

Selak joined the board in 2016, bringing over 40 years of experience in the financial and advisory services industry. From 2000 to 2016, he was a partner in the corporate finance practice of Ernst & Young.

At the executive level, Dan Farmer was appointed chief investment officer following the retirement of longstanding CIO Steve Merlicek. Merlicek had built a strong investment team, which included Farmer.

In October 2017, IOOF acquired ANZ's Pensions & Investments businesses and aligned dealer groups (ANZ Wealth Management). The transaction was substantially completed on 1 October 2018, with IOOF taking full ownership of the ANZ dealer groups, while securing 82 per cent of the economic benefit of the Pensions & Investments business. ANZ Wealth Management seamlessly fitted with IOOFs advice, platform and investment-management businesses.

Meanwhile, with the Murray Inquiry still fresh in mind, the financial services industry faced another round of inquiry and potential regulatory change. A coterie of journalists and Labor, Greens and Nationals federal politicians called for a Royal Commission. *Australian Financial Review* political editor Phillip Coorey outlined the genesis of the commission: 'Nationals senators who claim to have been ambushed over the bill to legalise same-sex marriage are planning to use identical tactics to legislate for a banking royal commission as an act of vengeance.'[1]

Pushed into a corner on the issue, Malcolm Turnbull reluctantly agreed to the Royal Commission. He told the ABC: 'While we regret the necessity of the decision, we have taken it in the national economic interest.'[2]

The Royal Commission into Misconduct in the Banking, Superannuation and Financial Services Industry was established on 14 December 2017, with former High Court justice Kenneth Hayne appointed as the Royal Commissioner.

The commission held seven rounds of public hearings. IOOF was one of the companies under the spotlight during the fifth round, which focused on superannuation. The inquiries revolved around allegations regarding governance and compliance relating to IOOF subsidiaries IOOF Investment Management Ltd (IIML) and Questor Financial Services Ltd (Questor).

During the hearings, IOOF faced several misconduct allegations regarding the failure to act in members' best interest, conflicts of interest, and inadequate governance and risk management. The nub of the inquiry was that IOOF had drawn on the superannuation trust's general reserve fund to compensate members for an 'over-distribution' from an IOOF cash management trust. The overdistribution was the result of an error made by the third-party custodian, a subsidiary of NAB. This had occurred under the auspices of the subsidiaries IIML and Questor.

Kelaher was summonsed to appear before the Royal Commission. Venardos recalled his thoughts on Kelaher's appearance on 10 August 2018. Venardos said the courtroom optics did not accurately reflect the facts of the case: 'The QCs doing the questioning had a fantastic grasp of theatre, and they created theatre on a daily basis that contributed to media headlines.'

Venardos said the commission's inquiries lacked substance, but also that Kelaher did himself few favours with his handling of the questioning:

~

I was concerned because the prevailing view was that he didn't show enough respect to the court and Hayne. That was the thing that really concerned me. I don't think it had any bearing on what APRA ultimately did, but I think it had a lot of bearing on how we were perceived, the reputation of the CEO, the reputation of the board and the IOOF brand. It did a lot of damage.

~

Kelaher's performance was poorly received by the media and the market, but it was not entirely unexpected, as he had displayed a similar manner before the Senate Committee of Inquiry into Financial Services in July 2015.

Following the Royal Commission's inquiry, on 6 December 2018 APRA commenced proceedings in the Federal Court against IIML, Questor, Kelaher and four other IOOF officers: the chair, George Venardos; the chief financial officer, David Coulter; the general manager for legal risk and compliance and company secretary, Paul Vine; and the general counsel, Gary Riordan.

APRA initiated the action due to its view that IOOF entities, directors and executives had failed to act in the best interests of their superannuation members. News of the court action wiped $900 million from IOOF's market capitalisation in a single day.

Within a week, Renato Mota was appointed as acting CEO, with Kelaher stepping aside. Allan Griffiths took over from Venardos as acting chair.

The Royal Commissioner submitted his final report to Governor-General Sir Peter Cosgrove on 1 February 2019. In response to the findings, IOOF implemented several measures to address the issues associated with managing potential conflicts of interest raised during the hearings. As acting CEO, Renato Mota assured customers and investors that the company was committed to doing better in the future.

Kelaher departed in April 2019 while awaiting the APRA court case's finalisation. He had led the group through transformative growth, taking IOOF beyond what had been imaginable a decade ago. His dealmaking acumen, visionary strategy and in-depth under-standing of the business had turned IOOF into a genuinely significant player in the Australian financial services industry.

Appointing a permanent successor to Kelaher involved a wide-ranging search, during which the board considered numerous high-quality candidates both from within the company and externally. Ultimately, the board was unanimous in its belief that Mota had the vision and experience to lead IOOF in its next phase of transformative growth.

In a statement released on 25 June 2019, IOOF chair Allan Griffiths announced that Mota—who had been the Group General Manager, Wealth Management—would be the company's new CEO:

~

Renato has a track record over a number of years in leading IOOF through a series of forward thinking, strategic initiatives. These include; the development of our advice-led strategy; the introduction of our ClientFirst transformation, which began in 2015; and establishing our Advice Academy from 2016, a goals-based coaching and business management program for financial advisers to help improve the quality of financial advice ... Renato's mandate will be to continue the change program he commenced as Acting CEO, to reshape our business and adapt our culture and capability to suit the evolving wealth management environment.[3]

~

Following the Royal Commission, APRA took IOOF and its directors to court. Federal Court Justice Jayne Jagot dismissed the regulator's case. Peter Rae/ *Australian Financial Review*

On 20 September 2019, the Federal Court dismissed APRA's application for a finding that IOOF entities, directors and executives had contravened their obligations under the *Superannuation Industry Supervision Act* (1993). Justice Jayne Jagot ordered that the entirety of APRA's application be dismissed and that APRA pay the respondents' legal costs.

Venardos said the Royal Commission's interpretation of the issues did not mesh with the eventual Federal Court ruling on the matters raised: 'Regardless of what Chris said or how Chris performed, those headlines would always be very similar. The [Federal] Court ultimately ruled that our decisions were appropriate and that the [Royal] Commission was incorrect.'

The judgment was a resounding win for IOOF and the individual respondents. In her ruling, Justice Jagot rejected the regulator's case: 'APRA's case, as will be explained, fails at the hurdle of proof . . . It was for APRA to prove the primary facts on which its allegations of contraventions depended. The way in which it sought to do so was fundamentally inadequate.'

Justice Jagot highlighted the inadequacy of APRA's case:

~

APRA has sought to pluck out of a lengthy and highly regulated process, two communications and, by examining those communications entirely divorced from their context, has alleged that IIML and Mr Kelaher breached their respective best interests and no conflicts covenants. However, when the entirety of the context is considered, both factual and legal, it is apparent that APRA's allegations are without factual foundation.

~

Her commentary also exonerated Venardos and Kelaher:

~

APRA's case against Mr Venardos for the alleged CMT Compensation Plan breaches cannot succeed for the same reasons as its case against Mr Kelaher. Again, I find the submissions for Mr Venardos compelling. The board was presented with a paper that was clear, apparently comprehensive, rational and reasonable. The board relied on the paper to reach its decision, as the members of the board were entitled to do. The conduct of the other members of the board excluding Mr Kelaher provides good evidence of what a prudent superannuation trustee director would have done in the same circumstances, which was precisely what Mr Venardos (and Mr Kelaher) did. The paper represented that the compensation plan had been formulated in the best interests of members. There was no reason for Mr Venardos (or Mr Kelaher) to doubt that advice. APRA has not proved otherwise. It has also not proved any of the other foundational facts on which it relies to implicate Mr Venardos in breach of his covenants.[4]

~

The external commentary was generally scathing of the industry, making it imperative for IOOF to regain the trust of stakeholders and the public. Following the Royal Commission, the company set about rebuilding its governance model, aiming to adhere to the best practice within the industry. At the board level, a key focus was entrenching new governance structures and introducing rigorous compliance standards. IOOF took steps to improve relationships with all stakeholders, particularly with regulators.

Even though the Federal Court ruling vindicated him, Venardos still felt pained by the episode. He stood down from the IOOF board and his other directorships. 'The way the justice system is meant to work is that if the justice system's working properly, you're meant to be put back into the same position you were in prior to the incorrect allegations. And of course, that's impossible in our system. That doesn't happen,' he reflected.

Despite what he went through, Venardos still felt great affection for IOOF. 'It's an amazing organisation,' he said. 'And if you think about it, the passion that I still have for it and that others like Roger Sexton still have for it should tell you that it's a pretty fantastic culture.'

He was proud of his time at IOOF and his contribution to the organisation across risk compliance and quality of advice as the risk committee chair:

~

I saw quality of advice as the future of the business, and having a compliance system in place that was sustainable going forward and allowed us to continue to work on the quality of advice being delivered to members. One of my lasting memories will be that we had an in-house team that conducted effective audits on the financial planners. We held ourselves up as having high standards, and the board was engaged in risk management and monitoring the risk culture. Those are my enduring memories.

~

Under challenging circumstances, Renato Mota's appointment allowed IOOF to reset after a torrid few years. With the IOOF brand damaged, its share price rocked and staff morale at an all-time low, he faced an unenviable task that might have sent even a seasoned CEO running the other way.

Insignia Financial chief executive officer Renato Mota (left) and board chair Allan Griffiths (right) reset the culture of the business and guided the transformation from IOOF to Insignia Financial. *Australian Financial Review*

CHAPTER 19

TRANSFORMATION
WITH PURPOSE

IOOF had been here before. Not in these exact circumstances, but similar enough. Faced with an exodus of members gripped by gold fever in the 1850s, IOOF had survived and prospered. IOOF had experienced the severe economic downturns of the 1890s, 1930s and 1990s. Two world wars and a pandemic had taken their toll, but still IOOF had come through. The massive transformation of Australia's economy and society during the post–World War II years and the advent of the welfare state had drastically changed the organisation, but had not extinguished its mission.

From 1846 to its demutualisation in 2001, IOOF was the little friendly society that could. It was spirited and adaptable. It was a trusted institution.

Then it shed its friendly society status, demutualised and successfully listed. Still, the critics expressed doubt. IOOF put its head down, ploughed on and grew bigger. The business model changed according to the needs of its customers, the evolving financial markets and the regulatory demands. The economy was strong at times and weak at others. Events like September 11 and the GFC tested its mettle.

However, the primary mission had stayed the same: providing prosperity and security for Australians. Since 1846, IOOF had helped improve millions of lives. In his history of the organisation, Geoffrey Blainey wrote: 'The Independent Order of Odd Fellows of Victoria is heir to one of the remarkable stories of survival in the history of Australian business.'[1]

Renato Mota understood this well. He joined IOOF in 2003 from Rothschild. Upon joining, he read the Blainey book and imbibed the stories from people like Tony Hodges, who hired him and became a mentor. For Mota, IOOF was not just another finance business. Its legacy made it special: it was an organisation with humble beginnings, a proud history and a consistent mission to serve its members and the broader community.

Born in Melbourne, Mota was raised in the country town of Traralgon by his Portuguese migrant parents. His dad worked long, hard hours as a builder in the booming Gippsland region, saving up money with his wife to buy a home and provide for their family. 'It's not a unique story, but my parents were blue-collar, hardworking people looking to build a life for themselves in this country,' Mota said in an interview for this book.

Mota's parents were great role models and gave him an appreciation for the value of a dollar:

~

I have always considered myself lucky to have strong role models in financial discipline, generally. And through my parents, I learned those skills. But very early on, I also realised that not everyone had that luxury, not everyone had that same role modelling in their lives, so I consider myself fortunate in that regard.

~

His interests in economics and commerce led him to RMIT University, where he completed his Bachelor of Business degree, topped with an honours year at Melbourne University. 'I always had an interest in global affairs, economics and finance. I was curious about how all this worked because I could see it affected people around me,' he said.

While still at university, Mota joined the ANZ international trade finance team. It ignited his passion for finance. 'When I came out of uni, I didn't have wealth management pinpointed as an industry I had a burning desire for. I'm unsure if I found it or it found me, but once immersed, I became passionate about it.' After three years with ANZ, he moved to NAB for two years as a corporate strategy and investments analyst, then took up a position as a corporate advisory manager at Rothschild. He was at Rothschild for almost two years when an opportunity arose at the recently listed IOOF:

~

IOOF had just listed and was ambitious. If you picked up a prospectus and did a bit of research, it was clear it was an organisation that wanted to grow, and that was attractive. Then, having met Tony [Hodges] through the interview process, it felt like this was a place where I could make a difference. When I joined in 2003, IOOF was still a small organisation competing with AMP, National Mutual, Colonial and BT but the culture was different. We used to joke that to work here, you had to be an odd fellow. There was always something unique about IOOF.

~

Under Hodges' tutelage, Mota worked his way up the ranks, starting in group strategy and communications, before taking on general manager roles across investor solutions and distribution. In 2016, Mota became the group general manager of wealth management. He was in that role for almost three years when he was tapped on the shoulder to lead the organisation in its hour of need, following the Royal Commission and just as APRA took IOOF to court.

It was far from the ideal way to step into such a position. 'It was a crisis appointment,' Mota said, who at 44 became one of the youngest leaders of an ASX 200 company. He recalled his feelings:

~

The reality is that the organisation needed stability and some leadership. The job needed to be done, and I was happy to do it because I believed in our mission and what we stood for as an organisation. I didn't want that experience [of the Royal Commission and APRA case] to define the organisation. I willingly accepted the role, but it was a challenge. And it's probably not the way you would've liked it to have happened, but it was this time of need, and I felt like I could make a difference and help us work through the challenge.

~

Mota had gained knowledge and experience working under four CEOs (Rob Turner, Ron Dewhurst, Tony Robinson and Christopher Kelaher) and four chairmen (Ray Schoer, Ian Blair, Roger Sexton and George Venardos). He had learned something different from each.

The former CEOs and directors interviewed for this book all spoke highly of Mota. Ron Dewhurst recalled that Mota was enthusiastic and thirsty for knowledge and experience: 'He was this really smart, young guy, working in strategy alongside Tony [Hodges]. He had a lot of excellent technical skills. But he also had a nice manner about him, grounded and personable.'

Regarding Mota's elevation to CEO, Hodges was fulsome in his praise:

~

I was so happy for Renato when he got the job, and I was confident that he could take it on successfully. He has a great love for the place, and he's very switched on. I knew he would have the interests of IOOF and the people there at heart.

~

Would Mota be the accidental captain of a doomed ship? Could he give IOOF a fresh start? IOOF was in good shape financially, but its reputation had taken a beating, from the allegations aired in the media in 2015 to the fallout from the Royal Commission and APRA's court case. The broader finance industry was in bad shape, and IOOF was among the companies that bore the brunt of the public's outcry.

Despite being disappointed by the media's portrayal of IOOF during the Royal Commission, Mota said it was a wake-up call for an industry that had drifted off course:

~

It became apparent there was a genuine disconnect between societal expectations and industry expectations. I say industry quite deliberately because it wasn't an IOOF-specific issue. It was an issue of the industry operating to different expectations. Whether it's IOOF or AMP, whichever organisation, they're full of good people who genuinely believe in what they do, yet there was a disconnect. That's the only thing that matters: we weren't delivering in a way consistent with expectations. So there were some great learnings from the Royal Commission, but it wasn't pleasant.

~

The Royal Commission fallout devastated employee morale, and some staff questioned the organisation's character. Adrianna Bisogni—at the time a former IOOF group general counsel—discussed the Royal Commission with friends who worked at IOOF or were fellow former employees, and recalled the disappointment they all felt. She said the Royal Commission upset many at IOOF because the organisation's self-image had always been positive: 'We had always been the entity tapped on the shoulder to take over others and then to have that reputation damaged for all those that bleed green—it was a tough thing to take, especially when that wasn't the IOOF culture we knew.'

At the end of 2019, Bisogni returned to IOOF to help uplift governance. She was appointed company secretary in November, taking over from Paul Vine. Previously, she was at IOOF for six years, from 2003 until 2009, departing immediately after the merger with AWM. She was fond of working at IOOF and keen to turn things around. 'We say IOOF people bleed green. And even though I had left, Renato knew I bled green. It's an organisation that . . . I don't know how it gets you like that, but it hooks you.'

Kelaher's tenure had brought unprecedented growth for the business. But that growth had incurred costs. The finance industry is highly regulated and scrutinised. Organisations must consistently meet statutory requirements, maintain appropriate governance, and listen to the concerns of a wide range of stakeholders. By doing all this, it preserves the social licence entrusted by stakeholders. Kelaher's relentless M&A strategy sometimes left the organisation's core governance capacities gasping for breath. As soon as one deal was done, the hunt was on for the next. This is not unusual for successful, fast-growth enterprises, but can lead to organisational fatigue.

Trust was at the core of the old friendly societies, and it remains fundamental for modern financial services organisations. Mota understood this as he set about stabilising an organisation rocked by four years of reputational damage and fractious relationships with regulators. He acknowledged that IOOF had hard lessons to learn, and that it had to learn them quickly and act upon them meaningfully to begin restoring its standing. IOOF could not move beyond its troubles without addressing its governance framework and rehabilitating its relationships with regulators.

IOOF met all the licence conditions that APRA imposed. One of the conditions involved the establishment of an Office of the Super-annuation Trustee (OST), a dedicated business function to support the superannuation trustees to fulfill their fiduciary obligations by advocating for member interests. Additional remedial actions included readying the adoption of all appropriate Protecting Your Super and Royal Commission recommendations, and providing $182.7 million for remediation and $40.4 million in related program costs.

After six months as acting CEO, Mota took over the reins permanently on 25 June 2019. Not everyone thought his appointment was the best idea. The main objection was that, as a long-time employee who had served under Kelaher, Mota could not objectively tackle IOOF's cultural issues. In the *Australian Financial Review*'s

Chanticleer column, James Thomson argued at the time that 'IOOF has failed to seize a chance to embrace cultural change':

~

The decision to replace chief executive Chris Kelaher—who this time next week will be in the midst of a Federal Court fight with the prudential regulator—with a 16-year company veteran who previously ran IOOF's wealth business might have been widely expected. But it should surely disappoint investors. That is no knock on the skills of new CEO Renato Mota, who has steadied the ship since his appointment as acting chief in December. And to his credit, he isn't shying away from the challenge at hand, telling Chanticleer on Tuesday he is ready to recalibrate IOOF and help lead the recalibration of the entire wealth industry. But it is impossible to ignore the events around Kelaher's departure, which surely called for an outsider to lead IOOF's turnaround.[2]

~

Thomson was not alone in his assessment, with others saying IOOF needed a complete cleanout of its executive ranks. While it likely never crossed the minds of the board, Mota's appointment was, in one way, a case of 'back to the future' for IOOF. He was the first CEO appointed from within the organisation since the 1970s. Before Martyn Pickersgill arrived in 1982 from IOOF's old rival ANA, it was commonplace for the managing director to come from within, usually rising through the friendly society ranks to take the top job. However, from Pickersgill on, all of IOOF's chief executives had been external hires. Mota did not have the advantage of fresh eyes, but he did have deep knowledge.

New chair Allan Griffiths proved a crucial boardroom ally in Mota's quest to repair and restore IOOF's reputation. While acting CEO, Mota initiated a management review and overhaul of the company's governance, specifically assessing the risk and compliance function. The goal was to elevate the governance structure to absolute industry best practice. The board supported this initiative and trusted Mota's instincts. Griffiths played an essential role in backing Mota internally and externally, especially in the media. His standing in the corporate community and his extensive experience at the executive and board levels provided much-needed ballast for Mota's mission.

The protracted acquisition of the ANZ pensions and investments business began when the senior management of IOOF was embroiled in Royal Commission hearings. Joel Carrett/AAP Image

Recent changes to superannuation laws meant the acquisition of controlling stakes in super funds now required regulatory approval. Improving the relationship with APRA was incredibly pertinent, as IOOF was acquiring substantial parts of the ANZ Wealth Management business, which needed APRA's approval.

IOOF's interest in buying the ANZ Wealth Management business started in 2016. In April 2017, despite reports that ANZ was not keen on selling to IOOF, Kelaher pushed the idea publicly. 'We've been asked previously if we are interested in acquiring that asset. The answer is: yes, we are,' Kelaher told *The Australian*.[3] The travails of the Royal Commission bogged down an already complicated deal, with both ANZ and IOOF having to contend with court cases, remediation costs and additional compliance requirements. However, acquiring the superannuation and investment parts of the ANZ wealth business made perfect sense for IOOF's strategy to grow adviser numbers and platform volume. The exit of the big banks from the wealth-management industry was manna from heaven for aspirants like IOOF.

The ANZ acquisition was complex and drawn out. On 17 October 2017, IOOF announced an agreement with ANZ to acquire ANZ's OnePath Pensions and Investments (ANZ P&I) business and the ANZ-aligned dealer groups for a cash consideration of $975 million, subject to a completion adjustment. On 26 July 2018, the IOOF Group entered into a non-binding term sheet with ANZ for accelerated completion of the acquisition. The expectation at this stage was for the deal to be completed by March 2019. APRA's court case put things in a holding pattern. The sale started looking shaky.

In April 2019, ANZ noted the disarray among the leadership ranks at IOOF. Speaking to the *Australian Financial Review*, ANZ's deputy chief executive, Alexis George, said: 'It's good that we now have a permanent chair [to deal with], but we just need to understand how we can deal with the capacity issue at the senior level. You have to remember there is no CEO or CFO or a head of legal we can deal with.'[4]

IOOF worked towards completing the acquisition through 2019. On 17 October 2019, it received 'No Objection' notices from One Path Custodians and ANZ and negotiated with ANZ a revised price of $825 million, down $150 million from the original agreed price. On 9 December 2019, APRA approved the applications by IOOF to hold a controlling stake in the ANZ-owned businesses OnePath Custodians and Oasis Fund Management. The acquisition of the ANZ P&I businesses was completed in full on 31 January 2020.

In approving the acquisition, APRA's statement signalled an advance in the previously brittle relationship: 'APRA's decision recognises IOOF's progress in strengthening governance structures and management of conflicts within its existing RSE licensees, in response to additional licence conditions imposed by APRA in December 2018.'[5] It endorsed the improved dialogue with APRA despite a contentious court case hanging over their heads.

Despite the challenges, business performance remained strong. Underlying net profit after tax for the 2018/19 financial year was $198 million, up 3.4 per cent from 2018, and funds under management and administration grew 18.7 per cent to $149.5 billion—helped by the addition of the ANZ advice licensees. Net profit after tax of $28.6 million was impacted by a provision arising from the PwC advice review. Positive net flows of $1.4 billion into IOOF's proprietary platforms and $520 million via the advice groups bolstered the company's stocks.

The advice review looked at 1200 client files and found examples of inappropriate advice, inadequate documentation, and fees for no service. It resulted in a $223-million provision for advice remediation. Mota said the review and remediation were necessary to uplift governance standards and assure clients. If IOOF were to be an advice-led business, it would have to correct past mistakes to regain trust and move forward.

Following the release of the Royal Commission's final report, the Coalition government led by Scott Morrison committed to adopting all its recommendations. IOOF was highly supportive of these changes. The most financially significant was the cessation of grandfathering conflicted remuneration to financial advisers, effective 1 January 2021. Remuneration under these arrangements represented $7.2 million in revenue to IOOF in the year to 30 June 2019.

While much of the spotlight was on governance and compliance matters, IOOF undertook a raft of divestments, targeting non-core assets. The divestment of AET Corporate Trust, Ord Minnett and Perennial Value Management signalled the continuing shift of the organisation's priorities from holding interests in boutique funds managers towards platform administration and financial advice. IOOF offloaded AET Corporate Trust for $51.6 million, Ord Minnett for $115 million, and relinquished its 52.4 per cent equity stake in Perennial Value Management. (IOOF did not disclose a payment for the divestment but said an independent valuation supported the 'consideration for the transaction'.)

Perennial had been integral to the growth of IOOF as a wealth manager. The boutique funds manager contributed immensely to the stature and coffers of IOOF, especially during the 2000s, with Mike Crivelli, Ian Macoun, John Murray and Anthony Patterson playing instrumental roles. Perennial's success signalled a coming of age for IOOF in its earliest years as a listed company. Without the expertise and credibility of Perennial in those early years, IOOF may have struggled to make itself an attractive listed entity. Despite tensions between the head office and Perennial's principals, its performance was a lighthouse for the group. Over the years, IOOF focused more heavily on the platform and advice businesses, while Perennial sought greater freedom to pursue its interests.

At a results briefing in August 2019, Renato Mota outlined a multi-year strategy designed to deliver IOOF to a position of industry leadership. This strategy consisted of three discrete phases: stabilise, transform and prosper. 'We have made significant progress to stabilise the business over 2019 and work continues,' he said. 'We have started our transformation with platform simplification underway and reinvention of our advice business. The completion of the ANZ P&I acquisition will complement this transformation.'

Rudderless at the end of 2018, IOOF suddenly looked stable, emboldened and ambitious heading into 2020. It was apparent that Mota was not a placeholder CEO—his vision for the company coupled growth with a refreshed emphasis on corporate citizenship and best-practice governance. The scale and footprint provided by the ANZ acquisition bolstered platform volumes, adviser numbers and funds under management and administration. In December 2019, Mota talked to the *Australian Financial Review* about his egalitarian belief in the value of financial advice for all Australians. 'I don't subscribe to the view that advice is only for rich people,' he said. 'We want to serve middle Australia.'[6]

In an interview for this book, he expanded on those thoughts:

~

The heart of the organisation has always been helping people in one way or another. And it struck me that some of that help can, at times, be very basic. At other times it's very complex. Not all the help has to be complex and there's a role for us as custodians to play in just helping people make better decisions. We committed ourselves to live our purpose of 'understand me, look after me and secure my future'. It's the key to our success and we challenge each other to bring this to life in our everyday interactions.

~

The focus on financial advice would prove prescient as the coming year unfolded.

With the company expanding in size, in the early 2020s, the company's head office moved to 800 Bourke Street, Melbourne. Shown here is the Insignia Financial reconciliation design launched as part of the company's Innovate Reconciliation Action Plan, which was endorsed by Reconciliation Australia in June 2023. Insignia Financial

CHAPTER 20

A NEW BEGINNING

On 12 December 2019, a cluster of patients emerged who exhibited the symptoms of an atypical pneumonia-like illness. Health officials reported Australia's first confirmed case on 25 January 2020. On 11 March 2020, the World Health Organization (WHO) declared the novel coronavirus (COVID-19) a worldwide pandemic.

Alongside catastrophic bushfires raging through Australia that summer and a global pandemic, several other factors contributed to a sense of doom at the beginning of 2020. Global economic growth was the weakest since the GFC. In the United States, Donald Trump's presidency divided the nation. Several international hotspots threatened to explode into full-blown military conflicts. But it was COVID-19 that dominated headlines and changed everyone's lives for the next eighteen months. No person and no business was immune.

Having already navigated IOOF through choppy waters, Renato Mota and Allan Griffiths now faced a seismic, once-in-a-century event. The pandemic brought two key challenges: prioritising the health and safety of IOOF employees and the community, and ensuring minimal disruption to the business. These challenges magnified as the pandemic unfolded over the coming year and state governments

The COVID-19 pandemic created economic disruption, with significant numbers of workers losing their jobs or having their hours reduced. Government policy measures, including the introduction of the JobKeeper wage subsidy, helped to keep many workers attached to their employers. Dan Peled/AAP Image

implemented lockdowns, which necessitated extensive work-from-home arrangements for all companies, especially those with offices in Melbourne, which endured some of the most prolonged lockdowns in the world.

The sudden economic disruption of the pandemic created a deep sense of unease within the community. Many people lost their livelihoods overnight. Others were no longer guaranteed ongoing work as thousands of small businesses around the country ground to a halt, with casual and part-time workers stood down.

In response to an impending economic calamity, the federal government rolled out the Early Access to Super scheme to support those severely impacted financially by COVID-19. The initiative allowed individuals to access up to $10,000 of their superannuation in the 2019/20 financial year and a further $10,000 in 2020/21. It was a drastic reversal of the previous policy setting for superannuation funds, but these were extreme times, with many facing unemployment and the prospect of defaulting on their mortgages.

Payments processed by IOOF under the Early Access scheme up to the end of the 2020/21 financial year totalled $743 million across 99,174 requests. IOOF facilitated 97 per cent of all platform payments to clients within five business days. Within the recently acquired ANZ business, 83 per cent of payments were made within five business days. At the height of the pandemic, the IOOF client service team experienced a 250 per cent increase in call volume, yet call wait times peaked at just ten minutes before quickly returning to just below five minutes, an achievement attributable to the ClientFirst initiative, which prioritised client satisfaction over all else.

James Camidge, who led one of IOOF's IT teams, recalled the intensity of the period:

~

We had a week to build something urgently, we were about to get tens of thousands of requests for COVID release payments, and we knew people had lost their jobs and would be stuck at home. Our team knew there were very high stakes. People literally wouldn't be able to buy food or pay rent. Some of our team stayed up all hours of the night to work on this automation, so our systems were prepared to pay the thousands of payments to our customers on the day it was available.

~

In addition, IOOF rolled out the Community Offer initiative in May, offering free financial guidance to those requiring it in local communities. IOOF gave advisers who volunteered at least 60 hours to the initiative three months of licensee fee relief. IOOF empowered its financial advisory network through Community Offer to step up and help those without access to quality financial advice. Around two-thirds of IOOF's 1300-strong adviser network volunteered over three months, helping consumers make sense of measures such as the JobKeeper program and the Early Access scheme. Community Offer cost IOOF around $2 million in waived licence fees and administrative costs and ran until the end of September 2020.

Rather than focusing on any bottom-line hit, Mota quickly saw the upside. 'This for many will be the first time they have had the opportunity to sit in front of a professional financial adviser and seek help,' he told the *Australian Financial Review*.[1] It may not have been in the best circumstances, but the pandemic encouraged many Australians to consider their finances seriously.

The 2019/20 financial year results took a hit as the COVID-related downturn significantly impacted the final quarter. Yet, considering the turmoil, IOOF's results were still respectable, demonstrating the underlying strength of the group. Statutory net profit after tax was $147 million, including substantial profit on non-core business sales. IOOF delivered an underlying net profit after tax of $128.8 million. The net platform inflows of $1.3 billion and net advice inflows of $730 million were solid, and the business reached a significant milestone with funds under management, administration and advice hitting $202.3 billion on 30 June 2020.

The IOOF leadership team recognised the impact of the pandemic on business outcomes and returns to shareholders. The executive team received no discretionary bonuses for the financial year. Mota and Griffiths took a 20 per cent reduction in base pay for six months from 1 August 2020. All other directors and the chief financial officer took a 10 per cent reduction in base pay for the same period.

Despite the scale of the pandemic's effect on the economy, IOOF's growth ambitions did not go into lockdown. Importantly, Mota's cultural reboot of the organisation galvanised employees and enabled them to proudly represent IOOF and serve clients and the community during difficult times. He told the *Australian Financial Review*:

Coming out of COVID-19 we have built an increasing level of confidence in our own ability to deliver when it matters, and with that has come a desire to play a bigger role in community and policy issues. If we do the right thing by the community and our clients, I am pretty sure that our brand will look after itself.[2]

The confidence identified by Mota was apparent throughout the organisation. After the Royal Commission, staff morale was low. Mota recognised this early and worked hard to rectify the situation. Because he was already a trusted and well-liked person within the organisation, he could get his message across quickly. He also had support from a steady and consistent board and a key group of executives around him. His mantra of 'transformation with purpose' went beyond narrow business considerations to encompass the company culture. He needed a unified workforce willing to back themselves to achieve the organisation's goals.

The federal government rolled out the Early Access to Super scheme in March 2020 in response to the COVID-19 pandemic. Major superannuation scheme providers such as IOOF were inundated with requests for help from customers. *The Sydney Morning Herald*

Through the IOOF Foundation, the company made a concerted effort to reconnect with the community, specifically supporting Australian not-for-profit organisations working with disadvantaged families, disadvantaged children and youth and aged care. Insignia Financial

Trish Briggs, who had joined IOOF as a community manager from NAB in 2011, spearheaded community engagement and out-reach programs. She worked closely with the IOOF Foundation and its officers, including Angie Dickschen, the chair since 2010. Its governance structure gave it a degree of independence from IOOF's corporate entity, with Briggs acting as a conduit between the foundation and the company. As a public ancillary fund, the foundation does not provide charity services but instead provides grants to service providers. In its first twenty years, it distributed nearly $20 million to Australian charities.

Interviewed for this book, Briggs said the foundation preserved a link to the organisation's friendly society roots while providing a meaningful way for IOOF to continue helping the community. 'IOOF set up the foundation to honour that past and develop constructive relationships with community organisations, especially with those helping the most vulnerable, including disadvantaged communities, children and the elderly,' she said.

Briggs noted that Mota's leadership brought a refreshed view of how different parts of the business, including community engagement and partnerships, could work together to cohesively achieve environmental, social and governance goals and business outcomes. 'I have so much respect for Renato,' she said. 'He's a people person. He's embedded a culture of being human and leads by example.'

However much maligned the financial advice industry had become, Mota believed it had an important role in helping all Australians secure their financial future. He wanted IOOF to be at the heart of that mission.

The 1990s and 2000s had seen the big banks move into the financial advice and wealth-management sector, with decidedly average results. One of the early instances of this trend was NAB's $4.6-billion acquisition of MLC in 2000. The acquisition signalled the beginning of the 'bancassurance' era in Australia, during which banks would add investment management and insurance revenue streams to their core business to create an integrated one-stop megamart of financial services for consumers. Financial advice was another part of this melange.

Under the cloak of the pandemic and lockdowns, plans were afoot for one of the most significant moves in the history of the Australian financial services industry. A core team around Mota was busy putting together a deal that had the potential to take IOOF to the next level.

In August 2020, IOOF announced it was acquiring MLC from NAB for $1.44 billion. The deal would see IOOF become the nation's largest provider of financial advice and the second-largest in the superannuation system, with $510 billion in assets under its control. It was a remarkable turnaround for a company that had faced such significant challenges only eighteen months before.

Some in the media doubted the wisdom of such a deal, and a few shareholders opposed it, mainly because they believed IOOF was overpaying for MLC and could not manage the integration profitably. However, the vast majority of shareholders approved the deal at that year's AGM.

'We acknowledge that there were some shareholders that were voicing disappointment on where the share price has been over the past month or so,' Mota told the *Australian Financial Review*. 'But the longer-term prospects that the MLC transaction creates for the business are unchanged irrespective of the short-term impact.'[3]

The audacious acquisition more than doubled the size of IOOF. It spoke to Mota's confidence in the organisation and his ambitious vision for the future. The acquisitions of the ANZ businesses and

In 2020, IOOF acquired rival wealth management firm MLC for $1.44 billion from NAB. Stephen Dwyer/Alamy

MLC provided scale, diversification and strength. It immediately elevated the organisation to a new level within the Australian financial services industry. Coming through the worst of the pandemic and effectively integrating three substantial businesses into one, IOOF was in sprightly shape. As so often in its history, it had been reborn. The emblematic green of its colour scheme once more signified renewal and revival.

Chris Weldon joined IOOF in August 2011 from MLC. Mota, then the general manager for distribution, hired Weldon for the head of product role. By 2018, Weldon was responsible for leading, developing and enabling IOOF's ClientFirst team in Hobart and then nationally in 2020. Mota appointed him as chief transformation officer in September 2020, with a brief to lead the integration of the recently acquired businesses.

Interviewed for this book, Weldon reflected on the transformation at the product and platform levels to serve clients better and on the challenges of integrating the ANZ and MLC businesses. For Weldon, the pivotal point in his journey arrived in 2018, when he moved into a frontline position, enabling him to see the client relationship from a novel perspective. Weldon was in a managerial role but needed to understand the client experience more intimately:

~

We were going through our change of our client servicing operating model, moving to our ClientFirst way of working. Before that, our operating model was more akin to a factory where tasks were broken down into specialist areas. The change to a ClientFirst approach saw us consolidate the call centre with the back-office administration functions, and multi-skill our people so that they could handle any type of client demands end-to-end, without the need to hand it off to another department or person. This meant if a client called with a problem, the ClientFirst operator could take ownership and resolve that problem directly with one touch. This was a very different operating model, requiring different ways of thinking from our people and a significant change in mindset where all our people in the system of work were required to take responsibility for client outcomes.

~

Weldon spent two years at the coalface, using his experiences and talking to his colleagues about improving processes and systems. Alongside extensive data analysis of client interactions, the insights of Weldon and his client service colleagues helped shape the ClientFirst ethos. This new understanding and the revamped processes held IOOF in good shape for handling the increased demands placed upon the organisation, especially during the pandemic.

Frank Lombardo joined IOOF in 2015 from NAB as the general manager for transformation, before taking on the role of chief operating officer in 2016. He spearheaded the ClientFirst strategy and played a significant role in consolidating systems and platform integration, especially at the technology level. Interviewed for this book, he said the organisation held a tremendous capacity for agility even in trying times.

'There is a nimbleness about the organisation,' Lombardo said. 'A secret sauce in this organisation is how we collaborate and work together to adapt to a dynamic environment. It contributes to that ability to deliver some significant change in really short timeframes relative to peers.'

He said the challenge of integrating the ANZ and MLC businesses while coping with the demands of the pandemic underlined the importance of the transformational work that the group had undertaken:

~

Those foundations hold us in good stead in terms of continuing to adapt to a changing environment. We had a clear vision of the technology capability and what was required to make ourselves adaptable. Evolve21 was the program of work that enabled us to move from the old legacy systems into that new platform. That was a monumental achievement for the business.

~

Adrianna Bisogni was part of the management revamp, returning to IOOF to take up the role of group company secretary after several years away. She had worked closely with Mota on the AM Corporation, Skandia and AWM mergers during her first period at IOOF, and recalled the camaraderie of those times:

~

One of my fondest memories was we would have the top floor in the IOOF building. And Renato, myself and Mark Blackburn (then CFO) would do the work and send the material out to the party we were dealing with, and then we'd kick the footy down the whole length of the executive area. It would be three o'clock in the morning, and we'd be kicking the footy around the office. Apparently, I was the only person who could kick the footy in a pair of high heels.

~

She said that, in many ways, acquiring a business is the easy part of the equation; the hard part is integration. 'With the ANZ and MLC businesses, there was a massive effort in digesting these businesses in a way that set us up for success, achieving those economies of scale and showing ourselves as a big player,' Bisogni said. In her view, the governance transformation during Mota's first two years in charge was phenomenal:

~

The whole governance uplift across the organisation demonstrated to the regulators that there was no ill intent in this organisation. We understand our responsibility to market and to the industry that our size brings. It was an astounding turnaround to go from a situation of the Royal Commission and consequent APRA action to acquiring a business the size of MLC. That you could manage a turnaround of that scale in that timeframe is a credit to Renato.

~

Towards the end of 2021, on the 175th anniversary of the organisation's birth, Mota and the board leaned into change and made another fearless call: IOOF would change its name. Following approval by 97.83 per cent of the voting shareholders at the IOOF Holdings Ltd annual general meeting on 25 November, IOOF changed its name to Insignia Financial Ltd. At the AGM, Mota explained the reasons for the name change:

~

The name Insignia represents a distinguishing emblem associated with membership and belonging. It strongly connects with our purpose: 'Understand me, look after me, secure my future.' This decision comes at an important inflection point in our organisation's transformation. We're proud of our heritage, who we are and what we stand for. Of course, this doesn't change. However, today, we can build on the past through a new corporate brand that captures the essence of our history in a more contemporary way.

~

Interviewed for this book, Mota expanded on the thinking behind the momentous move to leave behind the IOOF name after 175 years. He dismissed the suggestion that the name change was part of a strategy to distance the business from the troubles of the Royal Commission:

~

We have a longer-term view of things than that. We wanted to carry the flame of the heritage of the three organisations. Along with IOOF, the MLC heritage is equally strong; we're proud of that. The ANZ business can trace its roots to the old Mercantile Mutual, so the three organisations have a similar heritage, and we wanted to honour it in the rebranding.

~

The new logo deftly blended vital elements of the historic IOOF and MLC logos, including the stylised interlinked hoops of friendship characteristic of IOOF and the MLC nest egg representing financial security, while maintaining the iconic green colour scheme.

'The rebrand was a way to create a moment in time where we bring the three businesses together and create something everyone can feel they belong to, as opposed to the feeling of being taken over,' Mota explained. 'We wanted to unify the organisation while still remembering and honouring the past.'

The transformation from IOOF to Insignia Financial heralded the end of the long, glorious and, at times, odd journey of the Independent Order of Odd Fellows from a small friendly society in a colonial township to a billion-dollar financial services business of the 21st century. A new identity was embraced. However, that identity carried the legacy and spirit of 175 years of the Odd Fellows, from 1846 to 2021.

The organisation's DNA, always linked to helping Australians secure their financial security and wellbeing, was to live on. Insignia Financial was beginning a new journey, gently guided by the noble ideals of the Odd Fellows.

As seen on the side of the Insignia Financial office in Hobart, the company's new logo combines the traditional green interlinked circles of IOOF with the iconic MLC nest egg. Insignia Financial

CHAPTER 21

THE NEXT STEP FORWARD

The first six months of Insignia Financial involved significant work integrating the IOOF, MLC and ANZ pensions and investments businesses, focusing on developing and implementing its product and platform simplification roadmap.

One issue to arise in early 2022 was the need to address a Federal Court ruling that found one of Insignia Financial's self-employed advice businesses, RI Advice, had failed to ensure financial advisers operating under its licence acted in the best interests of clients. Despite the conduct occurring when ANZ owned the business, Insignia Financial accepted liability and paid the $6 million penalty handed down by the court.

Additional problems identified by Insignia Financial within the former ANZ businesses also led to client remediation increasing by $32 million, taking the total remediation bill following the findings of the Hayne Royal Commission to $234 million.

In October 2022, Insignia Financial completed the separation of the pensions and investments business from ANZ. The multi-year program involved 1257 employees transitioning from ANZ to Insignia Financial, with 638 commercial licence arrangements separated from ANZ and 589 applications separated or migrated from ANZ. Insignia Financial now had complete control and management of the systems that supported the former ANZ business.

Integrating the ANZ business had provided Insignia Financial's transformation team with a template for delivering a complex program to unite three separate business groups, ultimately providing better outcomes for employees, the business, shareholders and clients.

The integration of MLC Wealth was also progressing. In mid-2022, the next stage of asset management integration was completed with the development of two distinct investment streams. The first investment stream combined the management of diversified multi-asset strategies, while the second separated all directly managed single-asset class strategies.

Another important step in refocusing the business was the $135 million sale of Australian Executor Trustees to the ASX-listed Equity Trustees. A deal had been in the works since 2020, and the sale was completed in November 2022. The sale demonstrated Insignia Financial's intention to focus on financial advice and funds management rather than legacy businesses.

In a statement to the ASX outlining Insignia Financial's performance for the 2021/22 financial year, Renato Mota remained upbeat despite a challenging economic outlook: 'We delivered strong financial outcomes from the disciplined execution of our strategic priorities, and particularly from realising the benefits of the MLC acquisition.'

He was confident that 'integration is expected to be achieved 18 months ahead of plan'. He added: 'Simplification is key to unlocking the long-term benefits of scale, lowering the cost to serve, and translating to growth through improved client experience.'

Insignia Financial announced underlying net profit after tax for the year ended 30 June 2022 of $234.5 million, an increase of 59 per cent on the previous year. Statutory net profit after tax was $36.8 million, including discontinued operations. Results augured well for the future, but some figures raised concerns for shareholders.

After releasing the 2022 financial year results, Insignia Financial's share price dropped another 2.2 per cent. Negative returns from financial markets had led to a $5.3 billion hit to funds under management, advice and administration across the group.

Insignia Financial was already carrying the hit taken by IOOF to its share price following the Hayne Royal Commission. The workload involved in mergers and integrations also weighed upon the organisation. The generally depressed nature of the economy and the sharemarket did little to help the share price, either. Ongoing factors, including high inflation, rising interest rates and international conflicts, weighed on economic growth heading into 2023. Cost of living pressures and mortgage strain dampened household spending.

Despite the skittish reactions of some pundits and investors, Insignia Financial's strategy remained purposeful and coherent, with a concerted focus on making the organisation future-fit, particularly through digital technologies in the vital area of financial advice.

The financial advice sector was starting to get some long-needed attention at the federal level. Seeking to improve the regulatory framework around financial information and advice, the Morrison government commissioned Allens partner and superannuation law expert Michelle Levy to lead the Quality of Advice Review as the independent reviewer. The review was undertaken following the recommendations of the Hayne Royal Commission and focused on assessing the effectiveness of measures to improve financial advice. She handed down her final report in December 2022, by which time

The Morrison government commissioned Allens partner and superannuation law expert Michelle Levy to lead the Quality of Advice Review as the independent reviewer in March 2022.
Australian Financial Review

Anthony Albanese had become prime minister, leading Labor to victory in May 2022.

The review proposed a two-tier financial advice model. It recommended that the government overhaul regulation, paving the way for a wider array of consumer financial advice options, including digital and automated technologies (areas in which Insignia Financial was investing heavily), with less restrictive regulatory obligations. The overall tenor of the review was positive and aligned with Insignia Financial's commitment to better financial wellbeing for more Australians.

Midway through 2023, Insignia Financial Ltd announced it had completed the sale of its friendly society investment bond business to Australian Unity Limited through the divestment of IOOF Ltd, which was to be renamed Australian Unity Life Bonds Limited. The proceeds of the $36 million sale would be used to reduce debt. Another piece of the old IOOF was gone.

On 20 October 2023, by mutual agreement, Insignia Financial announced that Renato Mota would be stepping down from his role as chief executive, effective the end of February 2024. The announcement marked 20 years of service for Mota with IOOF and now Insignia Financial.

Insignia Financial Chairman Allan Griffiths said in a statement to the ASX, 'Over his time with the Group, Renato has been instrumental in transforming IOOF and ultimately Insignia Financial into one of Australia's leading wealth management organisations. His ability to create a purpose-led culture and execute a bold strategy in the face of numerous challenges, including a global pandemic, are marks of his outstanding leadership qualities.'

A little over four years earlier, on 25 June 2019, IOOF had announced that Mota would become its permanent chief executive after six months in the caretaker role. Initially, his appointment was met with scepticism by some, who said an outsider was needed to reset and recalibrate the business. But Mota had provided a centre of calm during a period of massive upheaval, leading the business through the COVID-19 pandemic, two industry-defining acquisitions, a national and global economic downturn and, ultimately, the creation of a new company.

Identifying and expressing the purpose of an organisation are two of the most significant tasks facing any leader. When he stepped into the CEO role, he knew that finding the organisation's purpose would be the key to its renewal. He remained steadfast in his belief that rather than scrapping the past, he could use it as a source for renewal. Mota had a genuine love and respect for the organisation's history.

'For many years, the Group was defined by what we were not—we were not a bank or a life insurer,' he said in an interview for this book. 'Over the past five years, we've re-established the meaning and purpose of the organisation: to look after all Australians through our expertise in financial wellbeing. We are much more than a product or a service; we are a like-minded set of people bound by a desire to look after our fellow Australians.'

At its core, IOOF had always been about helping Australians secure their financial wellbeing. Mota believed Insignia Financial was well-placed to carry that legacy forward, its sense of purpose and meaning renewed.

'Having spent the last five years building the foundations of a new organisation—Insignia Financial—with the culture, purpose, strategy and people to prosper for years to come, it felt like the right time to pass on this legacy to its next leader, one who can emphasise the growth opportunities and leadership position the business represents.'

As a professional, Mota had grown up at IOOF. He was one of those that 'bleed green'. The organisation had shaped him professionally and personally. He witnessed and played a critical role in its transformation over the past two decades. He was proud to have made a substantial contribution to the organisation. Asked which achievement most stuck out, he paid tribute to the people in the business.

'There are too many individual events, challenges and successes to mention. Ultimately, the organisation's culture, embodied by its people and their ambition, represents our most significant achievement. I joined a small, ambitious, friendly society and leave it as one of Australia's largest financial wellbeing organisations.'

The ethos of contributing to community is deeply embedded in the organisation's values. Here, employees help pack hampers for the annual Christmas appeal. Insignia Financial

Mota delivered cultural and organisational transformation under extremely challenging circumstances, garnering the highest regard and respect from his colleagues and the finance industry. Like many of his predecessors, he strived to build on the organisation's heritage while ensuring it continued to fulfil its purpose of helping Australians secure their financial wellbeing.

The past year had seen Insignia Financial achieve significant milestones, providing the foundation for unlocking future growth. The results of the 2023 financial year started to show the fruits of the previous five years of work. A strategic refresh aimed to improve the financial wellbeing of clients, deepen partnerships with advisers and employers, and ultimately build a safe and trusted business.

Insignia Financial is now in a strong position to honour and continue the legacy of the past and help Australians prosper for many more years to come.

NOTES

Chapter 1

1   Insignia Financial, *2022 Annual Report*, October 2022.
2   Byron Kaye and Paulina Duran, 'IOOF becomes Australia's top retail wealth manager with $1 billion purchase of NAB unit', Reuters, 31 August 2020.
3   The history of MLC is documented in Val Montagnana-Wallace and Jackie Blackledge, *MLC: Our Spirit, Our Story, Our Heritage, since 1886*, Bounce Books, 2012.
4   Geoffrey Blainey, *Odd Fellows: A History of IOOF Australia*, Allen & Unwin, 1991.
5   As at 30 September 2023.
6   Insignia Financial, *2022 Annual Report*, October 2022.
7   Insignia Financial, *2022 Annual Report*, October 2022.

Chapter 2

1   Living Histories, *Dr Bob James Fraternal Societies Collection*, The University of Newcastle, Australia, https://livinghistories.newcastle.edu.au/pages/fraternalsoc.
2   David Green & Lawrence Cromwell, *Mutual Aid or Welfare State: Australia's Friendly Societies*, Allen & Unwin, 1984, p. 31.
3   Daniel Defoe, *An Essay upon Projects*, Cassell & Company Limited, 1887 [1697].
4   Blainey, *Odd Fellows*, p. 7.
5   Penelope Ismay, *Trust among Strangers: Friendly Societies in Modern Britain*, Cambridge University Press, 2018, p. 19.

Chapter 3

1   'Local intelligence', *The Port Phillip Patriot and Morning Advertiser*, 8 October 1846.
2   'Domestic intelligence', *The Port Phillip Herald*, 23 December 1846.
3   'Domestic intelligence—Odd Fellows' dinner', *The Port Phillip Gazette and Settler's Journal*, 23 December 1846.
4   'Advertising—Odd Fellows belonging to the Manchester Unity', *The Port Phillip Patriot and Morning Advertiser*, 3 November 1846.
5   Blainey, *Odd Fellows*, p. 15.
6   Blainey, *Odd Fellows*, p. 15.
7   Bob James, 'Problems with UK and US Odd Fellow Literature', www.takver.com/history/benefit/ofshis.htm.
8   'Garryowen', *The Chronicles of Early Melbourne: 1835–1852*, Fergusson & Mitchell, 1888, p. 617.
9   Blainey, *Odd Fellows*, p. 17.

10 'Death of the Rev. Moses Rintel', *The Jewish Herald*, 21 May 1880.
11 Blainey, *Odd Fellows*, p. 29.
12 Blainey, *Odd Fellows*, p. 33.
13 Blainey, *Odd Fellows*, p. 28.
14 Geoffrey Blainey, *A Land Half Won*, Macmillan, 1980, p. 244.
15 Green & Cromwell, *Mutual Aid or Welfare State*, p. 45.
16 Green & Cromwell, *Mutual Aid or Welfare State*, p. 45.
17 Blainey, *Odd Fellows*, p. 67.
18 Blainey, *Odd Fellows*, p. 61.
19 *Friendly Societies: Final Report of the Royal Commission Appointed to Inquire into the Working of the Friendly Societies Statute*, Victorian Government, 1877.
20 Robert Murray, *150 Years of Spring Street: Victorian Government 1850s to 21st Century*, Australian Scholarly Publishing, 2007, p. 67.
21 T.A. Coghlan, *Labour and Industry in Australia*, vol. III (quoted in Jill Roe, *Marvellous Melbourne: The Emergence of an Australian City*, Hicks Smith & Sons, 1974), p. 122.
22 Jill Roe, *Marvellous Melbourne: The Emergence of an Australian City*, Hicks Smith & Sons, 1974, p. 90.
23 Blainey, *Odd Fellows*, p. 98.
24 Blainey, *Odd Fellows*, p. 96.

Chapter 4

1 'Oddfellows in session', *The Ballarat Star*, 14 March 1902.
2 Green & Cromwell, *Mutual Aid or Welfare State*, p. 45.
3 'The 1918 Strike of the Medical Profession against the Friendly Societies in Victoria', David G. Green, *Labour History*, No. 46, May 1984, pp. 72–87.
4 Green, *Labour History*.
5 Blainey, *Odd Fellows*, p. 115.
6 Blainey, *Odd Fellows*, p. 115.
7 'IOOF—The influenza handicap', *The Daily Telegraph*, 28 April 1920.
8 Blainey, *Odd Fellows*, p. 119.
9 Blainey, *Odd Fellows*, p. 118.
10 Blainey, *Odd Fellows*, p. 120.
11 Blainey, *Odd Fellows*, p. 122.
12 Blainey, *Odd Fellows*, p. 123.
13 'IOOF', *Shepparton Advertiser*, 12 September 1929.
14 Blainey, *Odd Fellows*, p. 126.
15 Blainey, *Odd Fellows*, p. 125.

Chapter 5

1 Philip Mendes, *Australia's Welfare Wars: The Players, the Politics and the Ideologies*, UNSW Press, 2017, p. 23.
2 'Local and personal notes—IOOF', *Shepparton Advertiser*, 27 May 1940.
3 'Value of friendly societies', *Williamstown Advertiser*, 7 December 1946.
4 'Letters to the editor', *The Age*, 5 October 1948.
5 Blainey, *Odd Fellows*, p. 128.
6 'New I.O.O.F. lodge at Dandenong', *Dandenong Journal*, 1 April 1953.
7 'Lodge news', *Williamstown Chronicle*, 24 September 1954.
8 Blainey, *Odd Fellows*, p. 139.
9 Blainey, *Odd Fellows*, p. 139.

Chapter 6

1 'Bradford History and Heritage', VisitBradford.com.
2 Blainey, *Odd Fellows*, p. 141.
3 Keith Campbell, *Report of the Committee on the Financial System* (Campbell Committee), Australian Government, The Treasury, 1981.
4 Blainey, *Odd Fellows*, p. 144.
5 Blainey, *Odd Fellows*, p. 145.
6 *IOOF Update*, November 1986.
7 *IOOF Update*, November 1986.
8 *IOOF Update*, November 1986.

Chapter 7

1 Peter Freeman, 'Friendlies limit rises', *The Sydney Morning Herald*, 24 February 1988.
2 Peter Freeman, 'Finance's tiddlers look a tasty bait for big banks—finance and commerce', *The Sydney Morning Herald*, 2 May 1989.
3 *IOOF Investment Update*, December 1988.
4 Blainey, *Odd Fellows*, p. 149.
5 M. Stevenson, 'Sons of Temperance', Museums Victoria Collections, 2009, https://collections.museumsvictoria.com.au/articles/2801.
6 Ross Greenwood & Andrew Stewart, 'The OST sticks its neck out', *Australian Financial Review*, 16 March 1990.
7 Greenwood & Stewart, 'The OST sticks its neck out'.
8 Cameron Wilson, 'Friendlies still good to investors', *The Canberra Times*, 20 May 1990.
9 Wilson, 'Friendlies still good to investors'.
10 Matthew Doman & Maiden, 'Vic friendly societies plan $3.7bn merger', *Australian Financial Review*, 6 July 1990.
11 Doman & Maiden, 'Vic friendly societies plan $3.7bn merger'.
12 Sarah Mills, 'OST's troubles are at heart of IOOF bail-out', *Australian Financial Review*, 9 July 1990.
13 Blainey, *Odd Fellows*, p. 139.
14 Peter Freeman, 'Societies may lose friendly image—dollar sense', *The Age*, 26 July 1990.
15 Freeman, 'Societies may lose friendly image—dollar sense'.
16 Helen Corcoran, 'Victoria's frightening collapse', *The Canberra Times*, 27 December 1990.
17 Ian Macfarlane, 'Boyer Lecture 4: The Recession of 1990 and Its Legacy', ABC Radio National, 3 December 2006.

Chapter 8

1 Ian Verrender, 'CBD—Stood up at the dance', *The Sydney Morning Herald*, 8 August 1990.
2 1989 IOOF Financial Group Annual Report.
3 'Victoria's crisis of confidence', *The Age*, 18 July 1990.
4 Michael Short, Robyn Dixon, 'Roper Ignored Trust Queries', *The Age*, 30 January 1991.
5 Peter Freeman, 'Friendlies who fight back—who stands to gain?', *The Sydney Morning Herald*, 27 March 1991.

6   Toby Darvau, 'IOOF friendly society may become life office', *The Age*, 12 July 1991.
7   Rod Myer, 'Moody's voices friendly society doubts', *The Age*, 13 December 1991.
8   Reserve Bank of Australia, *Annual Report 1991*, 'Financial System Surveillance'.
9   *IOOF Update*, no. 6, Summer 1992/93.
10 *IOOF Update*, no. 6, Summer 1992/93.
11 *IOOF Update*, no. 6, Summer 1992/93.
12 Deborah Brewster, 'Pickersgill calls it quits after 12 years at the helm of IOOF', *The Age*, 7 September 1994.

Chapter 9

1   IOOF staff newsletter, December 1995.
2   Jacqui Macdonald, 'IOOF retrenches its no 3 man', *The Age*, 28 April 1995.
3   Sarah Mills, 'OST's troubles are at heart of IOOF bail-out', *Australian Financial Review*, 9 July 1990.
4   Kathy Mac Dermott, 'Theme park in $60–70m float plan', *Australian Financial Review*, 22 March 1994.

Chapter 10

1   Stan Wallis, *Financial System Inquiry (1996) Final Report* (Wallis Inquiry), Australian Government, Treasury, 1 March 1997.
2   Ian Rogers & Simon Hoyle, 'Jostle for space results in mergers', *Australian Financial Review*, 25 June 1997.
3   Lisa Dowling, 'Over 20,000 OST policyholders accept IOOF offer', Australian Associated Press, 23 July 1996.
4   Simon Hoyle, 'New look IOOF ready to expand and take on banks', *Australian Financial Review*, 10 October 1997.
5   Joanne Painter, 'End of OST funds freeze takes chill off investors—Investment', *The Age*, 22 April 1998.
6   George Lekakis, 'Goodwill a bonus for OST's rescuer', *The Australian Financial Review*, 1 July 1998.

Chapter 11

1   Hans van Leeuwen, 'Friendlies try on different hats', *Australian Financial Review*, 8 March 1999.
2   Emma Tinkler, 'Australia's IOOF announce wholesale funds management', Australian Associated Press, 18 August 1999.

Chapter 12

1   Stuart Engel, 'Tower snaps up IOOF Trustees', *Money Management*, 26 July 2000.
2   Tim Boreham, 'IOOF makes one last sale', *The Australian*, 27 July 2000.
3   Tim Boreham, '$100m windfall for IOOF members', *The Australian*, 18 October 2001.
4   Jason Clout, 'IOOF lifts profit ahead of demutualisation vote', *Australian Financial Review*, 16 November 2001.

Chapter 13

1 'Ancient Independent Order of Odd Fellows', *Geelong Advertiser*, 18 July 1868.
2 'IOOF listing plans dictated by market conditions and acquisition', Australian Associated Press, 14 November 2002.
3 Geoff Easdown, 'IOOF listing on hold as war looms', *Herald Sun*, 20 February 2003.
4 'IOOF members upset at MD's departure', Australian Associated Press, 20 November 2003.
5 Stewart Oldfield, 'Loss of staff a risk for IOOF', *Australian Financial Review*, 27 November 2003.
6 John Durie, 'Static ... it plays on radio nerves', *Australian Financial Review*, 5 December 2003.

Chapter 14

1 Stewart Oldfield, 'Fund inflows lift IOOF results', *Australian Financial Review*, 24 February 2004.
2 'IOOF careful of its historical obligations', Australian Associated Press, 24 August 2004.
3 Angus Grigg, 'Rear Window', *Australian Financial Review*, 22 December 2004.
4 Tim Boreham, 'It's niche work if IOOF can get it', *The Australian*, 22 December 2004.
5 Eric Johnston, 'Plan to work money harder', *Australian Financial Review*, 7 September 2005.
6 Brendan Swift, 'Windfall for Perennial in $67.9m IOOF deal', *Australian Financial Review*, 6 October 2006.
7 Katherine Jimenez, 'Time to go, says IOOF's leader', *The Australian*, 5 January 2007.

Chapter 15

1 Paul Keating, 'Press Release No. 42—Proposal for merger of ANZ Banking Group (ANZ) and National Mutual Life Association (NM)', Australian Treasury, 23 May 1990.
2 Eric Johnston, 'IOOF is going the whole hog for organic growth', *Australian Financial Review*, 11 April 2007.
3 'IOOF appoints new CEO', *The Sydney Morning Herald*, 10 April 2007.
4 Matthew Drummond, 'IOOF funds inflow still lagging', *Australian Financial Review*, 28 August 2008.
5 Duncan Hughes, 'Mixed reviews for IOOF, AWM merger', *Australian Financial Review*, 25 November 2008.

Chapter 16

1 Jamie Freed & Sarah Thompson, 'IOOF medley doesn't have the ANZ zing', *Australian Financial Review*, 18 January 2010.
2 Duncan Hughes, 'ACCC warned about IOOF', *Australian Financial Review*, 23 August 2010.
3 Duncan Hughes, 'Finishing line looms for NAB, AXA', *Australian Financial Review*, 24 August 2010.
4 Duncan Hughes, 'Fears major players will dictate FOFA', *Australian Financial Review*, 20 May 2011.

5   Duncan Hughes, 'IOOF slams FOFA reforms', *Australian Financial Review*, 24 June 2011.
6   Justin Bailey, 'Minnows make a splash', *Australian Financial Review*, 23 March 2011.

Chapter 17

1   Sally Rose, 'IOOF still on hunt for takeover targets as underlying profit jumps 39pc', *The Sydney Morning Herald*, 26 February 2015.
2   Adele Ferguson & Sarah Danckert, 'Litany of wrongdoings at IOOF included insider trading by senior employee', *Australian Financial Review*, 20 June 2015.
3   'Financial services scandal: IOOF senior executives to front Senate committee amid cover-up allegations', ABC Radio, 3 August 2015.
4   'ASIC Media Release (16-221MR)—ASIC's inquiry into IOOF', Australian Securities and Investments Commission, 8 July 2016.
5   Tim Stewart, 'Shadforth integration boosts IOOF result', *InvestorDaily*, 10 August 2016.

Chapter 18

1   Phillip Coorey, 'Nats plot bank royal commission in gay marriage payback', *Australian Financial Review*, 16 November 2017.
2   Louise Yaxley, 'Banking royal commission: Malcolm Turnbull hates this inquiry, but it had to happen', ABC News, 30 November 2017.
3   IOOF Holdings, 'Media Release—Chief executive officer appointment and board renewal', 25 June 2019.
4   Justice Jayne Jagot, *Australian Prudential Regulation Authority v Kelaher* [2019] FCA 1521, Federal Court of Australia, 20 September 2019.

Chapter 19

1   Blainey, *Odd Fellows*, p. 148.
2   James Thomson, 'Chanticleer—IOOF should have picked new broom as CEO', *Australian Financial Review*, 25 June 2019.
3   Michael Roddan, 'IOOF poised to poach more advisers from bigger funds', *The Australian*, 28 April 2017.
4   James Frost, 'There's no one to deal with': Why ANZ is yet to sell to IOOF', *Australian Financial Review*, 6 April 2019.
5   'Media release—APRA approves IOOF bid to purchase ANZ superannuation licensees', Australian Prudential Regulation Authority (APRA), 9 December 2019.
6   Aleks Vickovich, 'AMP and IOOF: Last men standing or dead men walking?', *Australian Financial Review*, 27 December 2019.

Chapter 20

1   Aleks Vickovich, 'IOOF embarks on pro bono advice offensive', *Australian Financial Review*, 28 May 2020.
2   Vickovich, 'IOOF embarks on pro bono advice offensive'.
3   Aleks Vickovich & Lucas Baird, 'IOOF fends off AGM challenge, rejects critics', *Australian Financial Review*, 25 November 2020.

BIBLIOGRAPHY

✳

Along with the IOOF company archives and the newspaper archives of *The Age*, *The Sydney Morning Herald*, *The Australian* and the *Australian Financial Review*, the following resources have been important in the research for this book:

Blainey, Geoffrey, *A History of Victoria*, Cambridge University Press, 2013.

Blainey, Geoffrey, *A Land Half Won*, Macmillan, 1980.

Blainey, Geoffrey, *Odd Fellows: A History of IOOF Australia*, Allen & Unwin, 1991.

Campbell, Keith, *Australian Financial System—Final Report of the Committee of Inquiry* (Campbell Committee), Australian Government, The Treasury, 1 September 1981.

Cooper, Jeremy (chair), *Super System Review—Final Report*, Australian Government, 30 June 2010.

Defoe, Daniel, *An Essay upon Projects*, Cassell & Company Limited, 1887 [1697].

'Garryowen', *The Chronicles of Early Melbourne: 1835–1852*, Fergusson & Mitchell, 1888.

Gizycki, Marianne & Lowe, Philip, 'The Australian Financial System in the 1990s', RBA Annual Conference 2000, Reserve Bank of Australia, 2000.

Green, David & Cromwell, Lawrence, *Mutual Aid or Welfare State: Australia's Friendly Societies*, Allen & Unwin, 1984.

Hayne, Kenneth, *Final Report of the Royal Commission into Misconduct in the Banking, Superannuation, and Financial Services Industry*, Australian Government, 4 February 2019.

Ismay, Penelope, *Trust among Strangers: Friendly Societies in Modern Britain*, Cambridge University Press, 2018.

James, Bob, Fraternal Secrets (website), www.fraternalsecrets.org.

James, Bob & Weinbren, Dan, 'Getting a Grip: The roles of friendly societies in Australia and Britain reappraised', *Labour History*, no. 88, 2005.

Mendes, Philip, *Australia's Welfare Wars: The Players, the Politics and the Ideologies*, UNSW Press, 2017.

Murray, David (chair), *Financial System Inquiry Final Report*, Australian Government, The Treasury, November 2014.

Murray, Robert, *150 Years of Spring Street: Victorian Government 1850s to 21st Century*, Australian Scholarly Publishing, 2007.

Nobbs, R., 'The Development of Friendly Societies and Life Assurance in Australia', *Journal of the Institute of Actuaries*, vol. 110, no. 3, 1983.

Reserve Bank of Australia, *Demutualisation in Australia—Bulletin*, January 1999.

Roe, Jill, *Marvellous Melbourne: The Emergence of an Australian City*, Hicks Smith & Sons, 1974.

Living Histories, *Dr Bob James Fraternal Societies Collection*, The University of Newcastle, Australia, https://livinghistories. newcastle.edu.au/pages/fraternalsoc.

Wallis, Stan (chair), *Financial System Inquiry (1996) Final Report*, Australian Government, The Treasury, 1 March 1997.

Wettenhall, Roland S., 'The Influence of the Friendly Society Movement in Victoria 1835–1920', PhD thesis, School of Historical and Philosophical Studies, University of Melbourne, 2019.

INDEX